# Contents

# Introduction

This book contains over 700 activities for EFL and ESOL students, and is intended to cover all the important topics, functions and structures from elementary to upper-intermediate level. The majority of activities included here are short and to the point, giving the teacher an opportunity to provide on-the-spot practice, either when the planned materials have proved insufficient, or when a change of focus is needed. They can also be included in normal lesson planning. This is an invaluable resource for experienced and inexperienced teachers, and is unique in that the activities require no preparation. All that is needed is a quick look through the chosen activity to check the language involved and to estimate the time needed. *700 Classroom Activities* is the ideal tool for teachers who appreciate the importance of reacting to students' needs, as and when they arise.

## How to use this book

*700 Classroom Activities* is divided into four sections: conversation, functions, grammar and vocabulary. The activities within these sections are organised into categories that are arranged alphabetically, so that using the book is a simple matter of turning to the appropriate page for the topic in hand. There is an index at the back of this book, where the main references are in bold. There are also references to activities in which the topic is covered incidentally.

The activities fall into four main categories:
- The teacher prompts students with questions, key words or phrases.
- Cues are written on the board. This can either be done while students are engaged in the previous task, or they can be elicited during the presentation.
- The activity is instigated by means of a short dictation, or through the allocation of roles to individuals or groups.
- A project is assigned to individual students and they make preparations outside the class for an activity to be carried out in the next lesson.

The majority of activities are written as if spoken directly to the student. The language is not graded for lower levels because of the need to keep the instructions clear and concise for the teacher, so sometimes they will need simplifying. Instructions to the teacher are written in brackets. There is sometimes more than one activity under each heading. The start of each activity is indicated with a ▶.

### Grading

The level of difficulty is suggested next to each activity heading with shading on the corresponding level icon (E for Elementary, P for Pre-intermediate, I for Intermediate and U+ for Upper-intermediate). The range is wider for conversation topics, where the teacher can usually grade the language according to the class. It is more restricted for grammar topics, where structures are targeted at specific levels.

### The danger sign

There are some topics in this book which may offend particularly sensitive or easily embarrassed students, and others which might lead to antagonism between students with potentially conflicting opinions. These topics have been marked ⚠ . It is at the teacher's discretion to decide whether or not these activities are appropriate.

## Timing

No timing has been given for any of the activities; the size of the class, the enthusiasm of students for conversation topics and their aptitude for grammatical structures will determine how long an activity takes. It is also up to the teacher to determine how far an activity should go, especially where there is a list of questions or cue words which do not necessarily have to be fully exploited.

## Projects

These are assigned to students to work on outside the classroom, either for feedback in a subsequent lesson, or leading into a classroom activity. Many projects, and some other activities, require research on the Internet. These are marked (www).

## Focus

Most activities have two or more parts, usually with a different focus in each – pairs, groups, open class, etc. – and often using different skills. Where activities begin with questions, these are in open class unless otherwise stated. Similarly, feedback is held in open class at the end of activities. Unless a special focus is required, no specific instruction is given to the teacher to conduct a feedback session; it should happen as a matter of course.

It is always good to vary the focus, to have students working together in different combinations and, at some stage during the course, with every other student. This book encourages different groupings and students should get used to moving from one place to another, as well as mingling in the middle of the room. Wherever space permits it is advisable to have the seats and tables in a horseshoe. When putting students together in groups these should be as diverse as possible, with students from different backgrounds and with different interests sharing experiences and opinions through English. In mixed nationality classes there is the obvious advantage of being able to exploit the diversity of cultures for encouraging a great deal of information exchange. Students also benefit from the relative strengths in English that different language speakers have.

When teachers get to know their students well they will identify experiences and abilities in certain students that they would like to encourage them to talk about. There are stages to many activities which involve groups interviewing an individual. This is usually at the end of an activity.

Team games are an integral part of many activities and they enable the kind of friendly competitiveness that increases students' emotional involvement in the lesson, and therefore their receptiveness. They are also *great fun*. In team work, and other group activities, it is important to make sure that one student does not dominate, either by saying too much during conversations, or by giving too many answers during games. If one student dominates, ask him/her not to give any more answers until everybody else in the team has had a go.

## Written instructions

It is usually a good idea to write up the title of the activity at the outset, as a way of leading into the topic, and sometimes the first question to the class is about the title itself. Occasionally, however, the main point of the activity is intended to be kept secret until a later stage. In these instances, which will be obvious to the teacher, the title is not written up.

Where written cues are needed, these are kept short to reduce writing up time. A few examples and sentences require a bit more writing, and this can be done while the class is involved in the previous activity or stage. Students can also copy sentences as they are written, and these can include gaps to be filled in so that students are making decisions as they write.

# Conversation

## Accommodation

E P I U+  **My house**

▶ In pairs, tell each other about the place you live. Is it a flat or a house? Do you rent it? Describe your favourite room.

Tell your partner about an interesting place you have lived, e.g. *I used to live on a boat / in a tent ...*

▶ Brainstorm some different kinds of accommodation and think of an adjective to describe each one, e.g. *palace – luxurious.*

▶ In small groups, discuss the advantages and disadvantages of living in these places.

> basement flat, high-rise flat, hotel, caravan, cave, tree house

E P I U+  **Flatmates**

In pairs, imagine you are looking for someone to share your flat. Write a newspaper advertisement including information about the room, the flat and a contact number. Make sure you both have a copy of the ad.

Swap partners with another pair and role-play this telephone conversation.

Student A, you have put an advertisement for a flatmate in the local paper. However, in order to save money you kept it short: 'Room to rent. Call 020 876 1421.'

Student B, you are looking for a room. Ask student A about the room, the flat, the other tenants, the rent and any rules.

Swap roles, and role-play the conversation again.

What problems can happen between flatmates? (Brainstorm ideas with the class about these issues.)

> housework, money, TV, music, bathroom, telephone, friends, food

Imagine you went ahead with the tenancy. It is now six months later and you are fed up with living together. In your pairs, role-play an argument. Try to sort out your differences.

E P I U+  **Ideal home**

In small groups, design your dream home and garden. Include information about rooms, decor, furniture, equipment, facilities, location and staff. Prepare a short presentation to the class. If there is an artist in the group, get him/her to do some illustrations.

Have a class vote for the best house.

E P I U+  **Projects**

▶ Visit a stately home website and make notes about it to bring to the next lesson. Describe the home to the class.

▶ Find a house for sale on the Internet, print out the description and bring it to the class. In pairs, role-play a conversation between the estate agent and a prospective buyer.

## Animals

E P I U· **Animal talk**

In groups of three or four, discuss these questions.

| | |
|---|---|
| What's your favourite animal? Why? | Have you ever had a pet? Tell us about it. |
| Do you prefer cats or dogs? Why? | How do people treat animals in your country? |
| What animals do you eat? | What do you think of blood sports? |

E P I U· **Animal extremes**

In pairs, agree on an animal to fit each of these descriptions.

the biggest, the most beautiful, the most dangerous, the fastest, the slowest, the most unusual, the cuddliest, the ugliest, the smelliest, the friendliest

Compare your ideas with another pair.

E P I U· **Animal expressions**

► In small groups, explain these idiomatic expressions.

| | |
|---|---|
| He's a wolf in sheep's clothing. | I've got a frog in my throat. |
| I feel like a fish out of water. | She's got ants in her pants. |
| That's let the cat out of the bag. | He's the black sheep of the family. |

► In small groups, make up endings for these proverbs.

| | |
|---|---|
| The early bird (catches the worm). | Don't look a gift horse (in the mouth). |
| Monkey see, (monkey do). | Don't count your chickens (before they're hatched). |
| Let sleeping dogs (lie). | When the cat's away, (the mice will play). |

I'm going to read the real endings, out of sequence. Write them down and decide which expressions they fit. Discuss what the proverbs mean.

Do you have animal proverbs in your language? Explain some to the class.

E P I U· **Animal stories**

In small groups, brainstorm a few of the pros and cons of the following: keeping animals in zoos; modern livestock farming and pest control. In your groups, choose one of these writing tasks. Appoint one person to do the writing.

the thoughts of an elephant in a zoo, including an account of how he ended up there
the script of a conversation between a sheep and a pig on a farm
an account of the day-to-day life of a mouse living in your kitchen

## Crime and punishment

E P I U· **Victims of crime**

Have you, or anybody you know, ever been the victim of a crime? In pairs, tell your partner what happened.

**Punishment**  ⚠

In pairs, decide on appropriate penalties for these crimes.

> mugging, joyriding, vandalism, rape, shoplifting, murder, drink driving, manslaughter

Compare your answers with another pair. Then write a list of factors that make a crime more serious and those that make a crime less serious, e.g. homeless person stealing food.

**Neighbourhood watch**

There has been an increase in crime in your neighbourhood, especially violent crime and car crime. You are going to attend a meeting to decide what to do.

Prepare for the meeting in pairs. Discuss your ideas and make notes.

Pair A, you are:
The local MP – You represent the government's new 'get tough on crime' policy.
The local chief of police – You believe in zero tolerance towards criminals.

Pair B, you are:
A local youth worker – You want more money for community projects and you believe that prevention is better than punishment.
An ex-criminal – You are now working to help reformed criminals.

Pair C, you are:
The leader of the local tenants' association – You want a safer environment for the tenants.
A reporter from the local newspaper – You want find out the views of all concerned.

Pairs A, B and C, join to form groups of six. Role-play the meeting.

(If the class does not divide into groups of six, extra students can join pair C as reporters or local residents or act as chairperson to manage the meeting.)

**Big bad wolf?**  ⚠

Who knows the story of Little Red Riding Hood? Form groups with those who do not and tell them the story. (If no one knows it, tell the class yourself and then ask for a summary.)

Write a few adjectives to describe Little Red Riding Hood and a few to describe the wolf.

Here is some evidence that suggests the wolf was not the criminal but the victim.

> The wolf has been found murdered. He was shot three times, skinned and dumped in the river with his stomach full of stones. When Little Red Riding Hood was arrested she had the wolf's coat on and was carrying a gun. The grandmother has disappeared.

Work in groups of three. Role-play the police interview with Little Red Riding Hood.

Students A and B, you are police officers and you want a confession.

Student C, you are Little Red Riding Hood. Deny everything and give an alibi. Explain how you came to have the coat and gun.

Police officers, report back to the class. What was Little Red Riding Hood's explanation? Are you going to charge her? If so, has she got anything to say before she's charged?

**Capital punishment**  ⚠

Do you agree with the saying 'An eye for an eye, a tooth for a tooth'?

Work in two groups: those in favour of capital punishment, and those against it. Prepare your arguments for a class debate. Appoint one person to speak first for your group, and another to speak second. The others should help with the arguments and listen for problems with the other group's arguments. (Put anyone who is undecided in the smaller of the two groups. You could also ask a student to chair the debate.)

**[E|P|I|U]** ## Organised crime ⚠

Is there a powerful crime organisation in your country? What is it called and what kinds of activity is it involved in? Does it have any influence in government? Why is organised crime so powerful in some countries and not in others?

Work in two groups, A and B.

Group A, you are the leaders of the main global crime organisations. Brainstorm ideas to improve your power and profit.

Group B, you are the leaders of the police forces of the most powerful countries. Brainstorm ideas to help reduce the power of organised crime.

Compare ideas as a class with students in Group A taking it in turns to call out one of their ideas for students in Group B to try and counteract, e.g.

A – *We're going to smuggle more into the country through the ports.*
B – *Well, we've decided to increase security and the number of random checks at all ports.*

**[E|P|I|U]** ## Project 🌐

Visit a website on the subject of crime, e.g. the FBI's ten most wanted website. Make notes on what you find out for a presentation to the class.

## Culture

**[E|P|I|U]** ## Culture clash ⚠

▶ What are the advantages and disadvantages of life in a multicultural city? What does the proverb 'When in Rome do as the Romans do' mean? Do you agree with it?

▶ In groups, discuss the differences between cultures using these topics.

> festivals, family, weddings, religion, language, gestures, music, food, art, alphabet, clothing, famous people

▶ What happens when different cultures meet? Think of positive examples, e.g. the Moorish influence on Spain.

**[E|P|I|U]** ## Customs and traditions

▶ In small groups, discuss what you know about these festivals.

> Carnival, Easter, Guy Fawkes Night, Chinese New Year, Eid, Diwali, Christmas, Thanksgiving, Passover, Pancake Day

Find a partner from another group. Did his/her group know anything that your group didn't?

▶ In small groups, ask each other about your own countries, or other countries you know well. What is the national ...?

> dish, sport, dress, drink, music, monument

(If it's a single nationality class, answer questions about the UK/USA. Then ask students to work in groups and write sentences about another country. Allocate a different country to each group. Ask them to read out their sentences and see if the other groups can guess the country.)

E P I U **High culture**

► What cultural activities do you take part in?

In pairs, tell each other about what you do and the places you go, e.g. cinemas, theatres, galleries, museums, etc. (Ask students to specify films, plays and exhibitions.)

► Mingle with the rest of the class and find out everyone's favourite painting, building and piece of music. Note down the name of anyone who shares your opinion. Did anyone find someone with the same three favourites?

## Education

E P I U **My school**

In groups, tell each other about a school you went to as a child.

> where it was, a teacher you admired, a teacher you detested, a good friend, your favourite subjects, your best/worst subjects, a memorable day

Would you send your child to the same school? Why (not)?

E P I U **English school system**

What are the stages of the English school system? (Draw the chart on the board and elicit as much as possible from the class.)

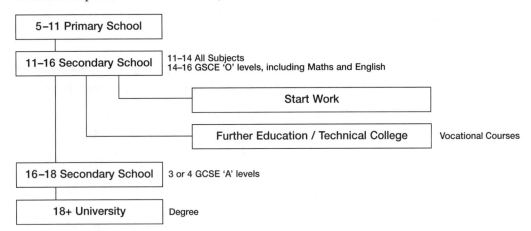

In small groups, compare the English school system with the system in your country, including subjects, fees, age ranges, degree length, etc.

E P I U **Discipline**

► How do you think disobedient and disruptive schoolchildren should be disciplined? In groups, decide on the best methods.

> corporal punishment, lines, discussion, expulsion, detention, parents, young offender institutions / reform schools, privileges, child psychologist

► In groups, tell each other about something bad that you, or somebody you know, did at school. What was the punishment? Was there anybody at your school who was particularly disruptive or delinquent? Do you know what happened to him/her in later life?

**Study skills**

In pairs, compare the way you study, including these categories.

> notes, filing, dictionaries, other reference books, speaking in class, asking questions, handouts, vocabulary learning techniques

In small groups, discuss the advice you would give to a student who wants to learn a new language. Agree on your top ten suggestions for effective study, e.g. *Keep a vocabulary notebook using different colours for different parts of speech. Ask the teacher if you do not understand something.*

**Class contract**

In small groups, make two lists of duties to help make a class effective: 1) students' duties; and 2) the teacher's duties, e.g. *The students must arrive on time. The teacher must correct written work within a week.* Compare your lists with the other groups.

Which duties should go in a class contract? (Elicit ideas and write them on the board.)

**Projects** (www)

Work with another student who would like to study the same subject as you. Visit a university or FE (Further Education) college website and print out some information. Find out about courses, fees, entry qualifications and other activities available for students.

## Environment

**Green manifesto**

▶ What are the main threats facing our environment? How can they be avoided?

In pairs, discuss these questions, comparing your experience of different countries.

> What are the most well-known ecological threats? Are people environmentally conscious? Is there a Green Party? How is the rubbish dealt with? What recycling facilities are there?

▶ In groups, write a Green Party manifesto, giving your proposals for an environmentally friendly lifestyle.

**Public consultation meeting**

A paper factory is planned for your town, which is very beautiful but high in unemployment. There are concerns from the local community about pollution and the destruction of an ancient forest nearby.

In groups of eight, you are going to role-play a public consultation meeting to listen to local views. (Allocate these roles. If the class does not divide into groups of eight, drop one or two of the roles.)

In favour of the factory: the mayor, a representative of the paper company, the building contractor, an unemployed person.

Against the factory: a member of the Green Party, an environmental scientist, a local craftsman, a local hotel owner.

Before the meeting, discuss your arguments with the people who share your views, considering pollution, visual impact, tourism, jobs and effects on other businesses.

Role-play the meeting.

P I U

## Eco-warrior

What is an 'eco-warrior'? What kind of issues do they fight for and how do they fight for them?

In pairs, imagine a motorway is being built through an area of oustanding natural beauty. How would you oppose it if you were an eco-warrior? What arguments would you make, and what arguments would you expect from the developer?

Role-play an interview between a journalist and an eco-warrior chained to a tree. Discuss the planned development, how long he/she has been there and what he/she plans to do when the bulldozers arrive.

## Fashion

P I U

## Fashion statements

In small groups, briefly discuss these questions and choose someone to report the group's opinions and answers to the class.

> Where do you buy your clothes?
> What is the most expensive garment you've ever bought?
> What is good and bad taste in clothes?
> Who is the best-dressed person in the class?
> Which countries are the most influential in fashion?
> What do you think of the fur trade?
> What famous designers do you know about?
> What is a 'fashion statement'?
> Do you ever make your own clothes?
> What piece of clothing would you most like to buy?
> What piece of clothing would you most hate to wear?
> Is fashion important? Why (not)?
> What do clothes tell you about the person wearing them?

P I U

## Uniforms

Why do people wear uniforms? Have you ever worn one? Tell us when it was, and why you wore it. How is a uniform different from a dress code? What is 'dressing down'?

Here is a list of people who dress in a particular way. Describe how they dress. Can you think of any more?

> B boys (Hip Hop), grunge kids, ravers, new age people, goths, surfers, punks

In small groups, discuss why these groups dress as they do. What messages are they trying to send?

P I U

## Clothes lines

In groups, discuss the meaning of these sayings.

| | |
|---|---|
| Keep it under your hat. | I wear the trousers in this family. |
| We'll have to tighten our belts. | She's got a bee in her bonnet. |
| Keep your shirt on. | He was caught with his pants down. |
| Put yourself in my shoes. | He's too big for his boots. |

Tell the rest of the class some clothes sayings from your country.

## Projects

▶ Write a description of someone you saw today, or an imaginary description of a famous person you'd like to meet. Then work in pairs. Student A, read the beginning of your description. Student B, ask yes/no questions about what the person was wearing. Then swap roles.

▶ Use the Internet to find a biography of a famous fashion designer. Make notes for a short presentation. Bring some pictures of his/her designs you feel strongly about. Work in small groups and show the others what you have brought and why you chose the designer.

## Food

### Eating habits

▶ In small groups, tell each other everything you ate and drank yesterday? Which of you has the healthiest diet?

▶ I'm going to ask you some questions. Listen carefully to each one. (Direct each question to a different student. Listen to the answer, then ask another student to repeat the question. Ask the whole class to write it down.)

> Are you a good cook? What is your speciality? What is your favourite fruit? What's the most expensive thing you've ever eaten? What do you think of British food? What's a typical dish of your country? What topping do you like on pizzas? Who does the cooking at home?

In pairs, ask and answer all the questions.

▶ In groups, find out how many different kinds of restaurant your group has been to, e.g. Chinese, Greek, etc. Which group has been to the most?

In your goups, imagine you are all going out for a meal. Agree on which kind of restaurant to go to.

### Potato game

▶ Take turns to name one thing that can be done with a potato, e.g. *It can be used as a paper weight.* If you can't think of an idea, you are out of the game. The last person to give a use is the winner.

▶ In groups, take turns to think of a vegetable and answer these ten questions without naming the vegetable. After each question, one of the others in the group will have a go at guessing what the vegetable is. Whoever gets it right wins points – 10 on the first guess, 9 on the second, and so on.

> 1  Can it be boiled?
> 2  Is it countable or uncountable?
> 3  Does it grow in the ground?
> 4  Can you eat it raw?
> 5  Is it bitter or sweet?
> 6  Do people eat a lot of them/it in the UK/USA?
> 7  What do you eat it with?
> 8  How big is it?
> 9  What colour is it?
> 10  What's the first letter?

### Rice

In small groups, make a list of different ways of cooking rice, e.g. *egg fried rice, paella, rice pudding.*

On your own, write instructions for how to cook perfect rice. Compare them with the others in your group.

## Food survey

I'm going to dictate one question to each person. Mingle and ask all the other students your question. Make a note of their answers. (Dictate each question quickly, but go through them two or three times so that students get another chance to take down their question. After the survey, elicit the results and write them on the board.)

| | |
|---|---|
| How much tea or coffee do you drink every day? | Do you eat health food? |
| Have you ever tried (Indian/Japanese/Greek) food? | How often do you eat out? |
| What is your biggest meal of the day? | Do you like fish and chips? |
| How much do you spend on food every week? | Do you prefer Coke or Pepsi? |
| What do you eat for breakfast? | Where do you buy your food? |
| Do you eat free-range eggs? | Do you eat a lot of chocolate? |

## Shopping lists

Work in small groups. I'll come round and write down the kind of meal you are going to cook. Agree a shopping list of all the things you need for this meal. When you have finished, look at the other groups' lists and try to guess the occasion they are preparing for.

| | |
|---|---|
| a Sunday meal for five people | a picnic in the park |
| a romantic dinner for two | a full English breakfast |
| a meal for a fitness fanatic | a child's birthday party |

## Sunday dinner

In groups of three, write a shopping list of the ingredients you will need for a three-course Sunday dinner, taking charge of one course each. Write the menu. Look at the other groups' menus and decide which meal you would most like to have. (In mixed nationality classes, try to make each group mixed.)

## Restaurants

► Work in small groups. I'll give each group a different type of restaurant. Create a menu and include starters, main courses, side dishes, desserts and drinks. Don't forget the prices.

> a steak house, a vegetarian café, an expensive French eatery,
> a motorway service station restaurant, a seafood restaurant

► In pairs, describe your last visit to a restaurant in detail.

> when and where, the food and drink, who you were with, the décor,
> the waiter, the music, what you talked about, the other people there

If anyone has experience of working in a restaurant, answer questions about the job from the class.

## Food for thought

In small groups, discuss these questions.

> Where is famine most common?
> Why does famine happen?
> How can it be dealt with?
> Can GM food help to avoid famine?

E P I U+ **One man's meat**

Have you ever eaten anything unusual? Is there anything which you think people should not eat? Why?

In small groups, discuss where in the world people eat these foods, and whether you would eat them. (Answers can be researched as part of the project below.)

> sheep's eyes, seaweed, bird's nest soup, snake, locusts, kidneys, snails, brains, tripe, flies, kangaroo steak, horse meat, shark's-fin soup, spider's eggs, frog's legs, black pudding

In your groups, put the foods in order from the most to the least pleasant sounding.

E P I U+ **Project**

Use the Internet to search for 'weird food', e.g. insects, ugli fruit, etc. Bring a printout and description to the next class. In small groups, guess how to prepare and eat it.

## Future

E P I U+ **One day ...**

I'm going to dictate one prediction about the future to each person. Mingle and collect the other students' opinions on your prediction. Note their answers. (Dictate each sentence quickly, but go through them two or three times so that students get another chance to take down their prediction. After the survey, elicit the results and write them on the board.)

> Computers will take over the world.
> Time travel will be possible.
> We will find life in other solar systems.
> Babies will be genetically modified.
> Unintelligent clones will do all the hard work.
> Disease will be eliminated.
> People will live on Mars.
> A comet will wipe out life on Earth.
> We will learn how to travel at the speed of light.
> English will be the only language in the world.
> There will be no more war.
> Everyone will live to be 200.
> The environment will be destroyed.
> Everybody will be dark skinned.

E P I U+ **Time capsule**

In small groups, agree a list of ten objects to put in a time capsule. It will be opened in a thousand years and the objects will show what life was like in the 21st century.

Compare lists with another group and ask them to explain their choices.

(Here are some examples. Use them either to prompt ideas or for discussion after the students have chosen their objects.)

> a training shoe, a bag of household rubbish, a bottle of mineral water,
> a tabloid newspaper, a music CD, a picture of a traffic jam, a cigarette,
> anti-depressants, decaffeinated coffee, a self-help book, a mobile phone

## My future

In pairs, copy the table and fill it in for your partner by asking him/her questions, e.g. *Where will you be working in ten years' time?*

| My Life | In 1 year's time | In 10 years' time | In 30 years' time |
|---------|------------------|-------------------|-------------------|
| Job     |                  |                   |                   |
| Family  |                  |                   |                   |
| Housing |                  |                   |                   |

## Geography

## Mini lectures

In small groups, prepare a set of questions about the UK/USA/Australia/… . Write questions about these things. Then take turns to ask me your questions.

> location, population, climate, tourism, minorities, economy, terrain

Work in pairs with someone from a country you don't know. Ask and answer the same questions, and make notes about the answers.

(In a single nationality class, write the students' questions on the board and give a country written on a piece of paper to each pair of students. They write as much as they can about the country, then read out what they have written for other students to guess the country.)

## Describe and draw

In pairs, tell each other about the most impressive mountain, waterfall and beach you have ever seen.

Sit facing each other and make sure you cannot see your partner's notebook. Imagine a beautiful scene, draw it and describe it to your partner, who will also draw it. When you have both described your scenes, compare the drawings. How good were your descriptions?

## Projects ⓦⓦⓦ

► How many areas of outstanding natural beauty do you know about in the UK/USA/ Australia/Ireland? Have you been to any of them?

Work in four groups. I'm going to give each group a country and some areas. Use the Internet to find out about these places, how you get there, what the landscape is like and what kind of activities you can do there. Prepare a short presentation for the class.

> UK: Lake District, Snowdonia, Skye, New Forest
> USA: Grand Canyon, Yosemite National Park, Niagara Falls
> Australia: Ayer's Rock, Blue Mountains, Great Barrier Reef
> Ireland: Giant's Causeway, Ring of Kerry, Cliffs of Moher

► Bring a map of your country to the class and prepare a short talk including information about these subjects.

> historical sites, beautiful places, the area you're from, the weather, the economy

## Health

See Debate on page 29 for full instructions.

**E P I U** **Keeping fit**

Who in the class thinks they are very healthy? Are there any fitness fanatics?

In groups, write ten pieces of advice for people who want to get fit.

**E P I U** **Health care**

In groups, discuss the ways in which health care has changed. Here are some topics.

> Old and modern medicine: How have medical techniques improved?
> Nutrition: How has what we eat changed?
> Institutions: How have hospitals and asylums changed?

**E P I U** **Medicine**

► In small groups, brainstorm the ways medicine has changed over the last hundred years. Compare the medical services in the UK/USA with those in your country.

► In pairs, tell each other about the last time you went to hospital or the dentist.

**E P I U** **Happiness**

Work in two groups, A and B. Group A, brainstorm things that make people happy. Group B, brainstorm things that make people unhappy.

Find a partner from the other group and compare your ideas. Agree a list of ten tips for a happy life.

**E P I U** **Health debate** ⚠

Work in two groups, A and B, for a class debate. (See Debate on page 29 for full instructions.) Group A, prepare arguments in favour of these proposals. Group B, prepare arguments against them.

> The state should not be expected to pay for medical care.
> People who smoke or drink should pay for their medical treatment.
> People who are terminally ill should have the right to die.
> Medical advances justify experiments on animals.

**E P I U** **Superbugs**

Do you think there will ever be a new pandemic disease? In groups, agree on the stages of a plan for dealing with an outbreak of a previously unknown contagious disease. Think about how to control the spread of the disease, identifying and curing it, and how to deal with public hysteria and the press.

**E P I U** **Science and health** ⚠

In small groups, discuss what these newspaper headlines might be about. What are your attitudes to the issues?

> Government puts vitamins in water supply    Human ear grown on mouse's back
> Scientists create life    Baby gets pig's gene
> Human genome mapped    AIDS vaccine too expensive
> Operation to separate conjoined twins fails    Ambulance men to strike

P I U· **Project**

Look up the World Health Organisation on the Internet and find out about these things.

> the latest information about a current health topic
> the life expectancy for men and women in your country
> your country's annual health expenditure

In class, work in groups and share the information you have found. (Some other issues that you might like to suggest for research are clean water, tobacco, and nutrition.)

## Heroes and heroines

P I U· **My hero**

What makes someone a hero? Who do you look up to in your family? Did you have a hero at school? Tell us about him/her. Can you think of any anti-heroes?

Think of a famous hero and imagine you are that person. Stand at the front of the class and answer the students' questions. You can only answer 'yes' or 'no'. They will try to guess who you are. (Ask for volunteers, and if they can't think of a hero give them one of these.)

> Mahatma Gandhi, James Bond, Nelson Mandela, Superman, Robin Hood,
> Bob Marley, Princess Diana, Che Guevara, Neil Armstrong, Mother Theresa,
> Abraham Lincoln, Leonardo da Vinci, Joan of Arc, Martin Luther King

P I U· **Balloon debate**

(Elicit the names of two historically important people. Then draw a picture of a balloon on the board, with someone jumping out of it.)

Work in two groups. (Allocate one of the important people to each group.) The balloon has a leak and it can only carry one person. Convince me that your person should be the one to survive. Why is he/she more useful to the human race than the other person? Discuss your arguments and take turns to present them. I'll decide who has to jump.

Work in groups of five for another balloon debate. Each choose a famous person and prepare the reasons why you should stay and the others should jump. When you have finished, vote for the winner.

(Variation: This can be played with professions instead of individuals, e.g. lawyer, doctor.)

## History

 **Britain**

In small groups, discuss what you know about these areas of British history. Appoint a secretary to make notes.

> invaders, colonialism, revolution, imperialism,
> kings and queens, the First and Second World Wars

Work with a partner from another group and compare notes.

**Rewriting history**

In groups, brainstorm some important events in the history of the world. Discuss how things might be different nowadays if the events had not happened, or had turned out differently, e.g. *If the Spanish Armada had succeeded in invading England in 1588, Britain would be a Spanish-speaking country.*

**Monuments**

Work in groups. Choose a famous historical place you know well and tell your group about it. Here are some useful expressions.

| It is in ... It was built by ... They used to ... It was used for ... |
| --- |

**My country**

► In pairs, each choose a country you know well and tell your partner about it. Include these subjects.

| prehistory, ancient people, unification, religion, politics, trade, colonialism and imperialism, heroes and anti-heroes, revolution |
| --- |

(If the class is mixed nationality, put them in small groups to ask each other questions about their own countries using these words.)

| When? Who? Where? Why? How? What? How long? |
| --- |

**Epochs**

► In groups, discuss the advantages and disadvantages of these eras in world history.

| Roman Empire, European imperialism, discovery of America, Industrial Revolution |
| --- |

► In groups, try to agree on the three most important people in the history of the world. Then put these people in order of importance.

| Winston Churchill, William Shakespeare, Alexander the Great, Julius Caesar, Karl Marx, Abraham Lincoln, Buddha, Cleopatra, Joseph Stalin, Albert Einstein |
| --- |

**Projects** (www)

► Use the Internet to identify five positive and five negative outcomes from one of the historical periods in Epochs, above.

► Think of a world famous monument you would like to visit and look up some of the holidays on offer, either in the press or on the Internet. Bring an advert to the next lesson. In groups, try to convince the other students that your idea for a holiday is the best.

► In groups of three or four, use the Internet to find out about one of the seven wonders of the ancient world. Work with another group. Tell them what you found out.

| Pyramids of Egypt, Pharos of Alexandria, Hanging Gardens of Babylon, Temple of Artemis, Statue of Zeus, Mausoleum at Halicarnassus, Colossus of Rhodes |
| --- |

In your groups, what do you think are the 'seven wonders' of the modern world?

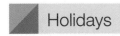

## Holidays

P I U+ **My holiday**

In pairs, use these expressions to ask questions about each other's last and next holiday.

Where? What? When? How long? Who with? How? Why? How far? How much? What else?

Whose partner had a particularly interesting holiday? Tell us about it.

P I U+ **Advice for travellers**

What advice would you give to someone going on holiday to your country?

Work in small groups of students who all know a particular city. (Ideally, different groups work on different cities.) Write a list of your top ten attractions for a visiting friend, including famous places and some that tourists don't know about.

P I U+ **Tourist alphabet**

I'll name a country beginning with the letter A. The first student will tell me the capital city, and then name a country beginning with B, and so on. If you can't think of a country or the capital, you are out of the game. The winner is the last student still playing.

P I U+ **Family holiday**

► Work in groups of six. You are members of the same family and are going on holiday together, but you each have a very different idea about the kind of holiday you want.

Role-play this discussion.

Grandma: not abroad!
Mum: sightseeing, museums
Daughter, 16: a spiritual retreat

Dad: sun, sea and sand
Son, 18: mountaineering/adventure
Son/Daughter, 7: theme park

► I'm going to give you some ideas for unusual holidays. Work in two groups, A and B. Group A, brainstorm as many advantages as possible. Group B, brainstorm as many disadvantages as possible.

mushroom picking, Antarctic exploration, swimming with sharks, cheese making, murder mystery weekend, battle re-enactment

Work in pairs with someone from the other group to choose which holiday to go on. Student A, try to agree on a holiday with Student B. Student B, tell Student A all the disadvantages you can see with each holiday. You have to agree on a holiday to go on.

P I U+ **Budgets**

In small groups, you are going on holiday together. I'll give each group a budget. You must agree the details of your holiday, e.g. destination, transport, food, accommodation and entertainment. You *must* keep to your budget.

(For the poorest group, estimate how much they'll need for a hitch-hiking and camping trip, for example. For the richest group, make sure that they've got more than they could possible spend.)

Now imagine you are on your holiday and write a postcard.

Now imagine you are back from your holiday. Compare your experiences with those of a student from another group.

### Adventure holidays

Work in groups of four. Imagine you have each just got back from a different adventure holiday. Here are the four holidays; decide where you went and tell each other what you did and saw.

> the Amazon, the Himalayas, Siberia, the Sahara

If you have been on an adventure holiday, e.g. whitewater rafting, tell your group about it.

### Projects

▶ Visit a travel agent's website and get some information about a variety of different types of holiday. Work in small groups to choose your favourite holiday. Write at least five questions you would want to ask before buying the holiday, e.g. *Is transport provided from the airport to the hotel?*

▶ Use the Internet to find out about holidays in the UK/USA/Australia/Ireland ... . Download a map of the country. Bring the map and the holiday information to class and work in small groups to plan an itinerary and a budget for a two-week trip.

▶ Bring some holiday photos to class and tell other students about them.

## Leisure

### Hobbies

▶ (Arrange the students so that they are standing/sitting in a circle. Stand in the middle. Ask each of these questions to individual students at random. After they answer it, tell them to repeat the question to the next student and make a note of the student's answer. Indicate that they should continue the chain so the question progresses around the class. Meanwhile, introduce the other questions so that in the end there are lots of questions moving around the class.)

> What sports do you play, if any?
> How much time do you spend watching TV?
> Have you got a hobby?
> What hobby would you like to take up?
> What do you do on Sunday afternoons?
> How much free time do you have?
> What do you read for enjoyment?
> What hobbies did you use to have as a child?
> When and where did you last go to the seaside?
> What are the main leisure activities in your family?

Turn your notes into full sentences, e.g. *Maria wants to take up hang gliding.*

▶ In small groups, discuss these questions.

> What are the main leisure activities in the UK/USA and in your country?
> What about other countries?
> What do you understand by the expressions 'quality time', the 'work ethic' and the 'leisure society'?
> How much quality time do you get?
> What do you think is the right balance between work and play?

## Leisure survey

In small groups, find out who ...

watches the most TV, has the most interesting hobby,
has had the most hobbies, has been a collector of something

## Music

▶ Listen to the following questions and write your answers on a piece of paper. When you have finished, work in small groups and ask each other the same questions using your answers as prompts.

| | |
|---|---|
| Name four instruments in an orchestra. | How often do you dance? |
| Write two adjectives to describe music. | What was the first record you bought? |
| What subjects are most lyrics about? | What was the last tune you heard? |
| What do you know about the Beatles? | What kind of audio equipment have you got? |
| Describe an instrument from your country. | What's your first memory of music? |
| Describe a concert you have been to. | What's a didgeridoo? |

▶ Work in small groups. Tell the rest of the group about a famous musician or singer who you admire. If there are any musicians in your group, find out who they look up to.

▶ In groups, discuss these kinds of music and the people who enjoy them.

classical, heavy metal, techno, folk, church/choir, boy band, traditional jazz, modern jazz, country & western, Afro–Latin, punk/thrash/grunge, Hip Hop

(If there are any musicians in the class, put them in groups with non-musicians to answer questions beginning with the following words.)

What? How long? Why? Where? How much? Who? How? When? Which?

## Island records

Imagine you have to spend the next ten years on a desert island. You can choose five songs, two books and one luxury item, which cannot be a means of communication.
In small groups, tell each other about your choices and explain why each is special to you.

## Experts

On a piece of paper, write the following three things: something you are good at, something you are hopeless at and something you'd like to learn, e.g. *DIY, wine making, to play the guitar.*

Swap papers with a partner. Find out as much information about your partner's answers as possible.

(Invite two or three students to prepare a lecture about their area of expertise for the next lesson. Have a question and answer session at the end.)

## Projects

▶ Do you have a favourite pop artist? What's your favourite English-language song? Choose an English-language song to bring to the next lesson. Prepare some questions about the lyrics, to test the class.

▶ Research evening classes available in your local area. Choose a course you would like to join. In the next lesson report back to the class telling us when and where the course is and why it interests you.

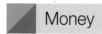

## Money

E P I U· **Money talks**

▶ In groups of three, discuss these questions. (If possible, group students from different countries.)

> What is the currency in your country?
> What is the exchange rate with the Euro / the US dollar?
> What's the rate of income tax and VAT in your country?
> How would society work without money?
> Do you think poor countries should be required to pay their debts to the rich countries?
> The world's richest three men have more money between them than the world's poorest sixty countries – should there be a redistribution? How?

▶ In groups, brainstorm one advantage and one disadvantage for each of these things. (Read them out, giving students a few minutes to discuss each one.)

> banks, credit cards, being rich, having a mortgage, pension schemes, direct debit

▶ In groups, brainstorm some differences between rich countries and poor countries. Choose three of the differences you came up with and agree the best way of making things more equal.

E P I U· **Bills**

In pairs, make a list of all the regular bills you can think of, e.g. electricity, gas, water, community charge, etc. Discuss which you think you could reduce, and how.

In your country, what does an electricity company do when someone doesn't pay their bill? Imagine you haven't paid your bill for six months. Role-play this conversation with your partner.

Student A, you are a bailiff and you are here to take property to the value of the unpaid bill. This will be kept until the bill, and the storage fee, is paid. There is also a fee for the bailiff's services. You are just doing your job.

Student B, you are a single parent and unemployed. Explain your situation to the bailiff. Try to come to some arrangement with the bailiff.

What arrangements did you come to?

E P I U· **Making money**

In small groups, brainstorm ways of getting rich, e.g. marrying into money, winning the lottery, buying a racehorse. Make a list of your top five.

Swap lists with another group. Decide whether you would support the other group's ideas and whether any are illegal or immoral. Mark the list accordingly and return it.

In your groups, choose your favourite money-making idea and make a list of arguments to persuade someone to go into business with you as a partner.

E P I U· **Inventors**

In pairs, invent an object – the stranger, the better – which you think will be useful to people. Make some sketches and write a brief description to explain it, e.g. *This is a pedal-powered computer that will give you exercise while you work.*

Team up with another pair. Each pair takes turns to play the role of the bank managers. Try to persuade the bank managers to lend you the money to produce your invention.

P | I | U **Hard sell**

In pairs, think of arguments to persuade people to buy these objects, e.g. empty coke can –
*You could use this as a vase.*

> a snowball, a dirty comb, one sock, a used teabag, a broken plate, cold fish and chips,
> a clock with no hands, a house with no roof, a bucket with a hole, a piece of string

(Invite volunteers to try to persuade the class of the value of each object.)

P | I | U **Sayings**

In small groups, discuss what these sayings mean. Do you agree or disagree?

> You can't buy love.                          Property is theft.
> Money talks.                                 Time is money.
> Money makes the world go around.             He who pays the piper calls the tune.
> A fool and his money are soon parted.        Money is the root of all evil.

Tell the rest of the class some money sayings from your country.

## Monologues

P | I | U **Mini-presentations**

You each have one minute to talk about the topic I give you. You must not hesitate, repeat
words or deviate from the topic. If you do, another student can challenge you and take
over the topic. Whoever is talking at the end of the minute gets a point. (You can relax the
rules by, for example, only banning repetition of nouns, or giving the talker two lives.)

> pets, music, parties, TV, bears, wine, cars, grammar, London, clothes, computers,
> smoking, pasta, work, the teacher, James Bond, the weather, radio, America

P | I | U **Twenty-second topics**

Work in small groups. Take turns to talk about the topic I give you for twenty seconds,
without stopping.

> my room, fun, my friend, this room, danger, cornflakes, rubbish, oranges, snow,
> holidays, money, animals, sport, furniture, coffee, astrology, the Queen, soap

(Variation: Each group chooses the topics and writes them on small pieces of paper, which
they put in a pile in the middle of another group.)

P | I | U **Keep talking**

Take turns to continue these monologues for as long as possible (up to a maximum of
three minutes).

> I always feel good when ...          The best time of day is ...
> It's a long time since ...           I prefer ...
> When I was young ...                 In England ...
> I wish ...                           There's nothing wrong with ...
> I'm proud of ...                     When I drink tea, I ...

## Accepting a role

Write a few unusual conversation openers. In pairs, take turns to read out your openers. Your partner has to respond in a convincing way, e.g. A – *I didn't know you could knit.* B – *(Knitting) Oh well, it's just a scarf. Nothing complicated.*

(Here are some possible openers.)

> Is that your baby? He's an absolute angel.
> I didn't know you did Tai Chi.
> Hi! Have you caught any fish yet?
> You never told me you had a pet tarantula.
> So you've started smoking cigars again.

## Speech ⚠

In small groups, take turns to make a short speech as one of these people.

> Oscar winner, best man, mourner, dictator, CEO (Chief Executive Officer), NRA (National Rifle Association) guest speaker, king/queen, television evangelist

## Noughts and crosses

Work in two teams to play noughts and crosses. (Explain how the teams take turns to place their mark – a nought or a cross – in a square of their choice, the winner being the first to create a straight line of three squares in any direction.) Take turns to choose a square. To win it you have to talk about the topic in that square for twenty seconds.

(If necessary, pre-teach these location expressions: *in the middle, at the top/bottom, on the left/right.*)

| my clothes | alcohol | war |
|---|---|---|
| police | mum | dogs |
| London | tea | music |

| school | time | happiness |
|---|---|---|
| bed | cars | birds |
| fruit | Canada | the sea |

## Talking with a purpose

I'll give each student a topic. In groups of three, have a conversation. Each of you should try to turn the conversation towards your topic.

> your favourite soap opera, roast chicken, tennis, astrology, the British Royal Family, the weather, your favourite recipe, a film you've just seen, your favourite holiday destination, a current news story, your favourite book when you were young

Which of you managed to dominate the conversation?

# Newspapers

P | I | U· **The press**

In groups, discuss these questions.

> What are the main stories in the press these days?
> What are the differences between the tabloids and the quality dailies in the UK/USA?
> Are there similar types of paper in your country?
> Are newspapers free from government influence in the UK/USA and in your country?
> What political views do different newspapers have in your country?
> Do you think newspapers should be smaller?

P | I | U· **Freedom from the press**

Tell me a few celebrities who are always in the news. What kinds of things are written about them? In groups, write some typical headlines, e.g. *Exclusive! The wedding photos they tried to ban!*

In the same groups, discuss your opinions about the freedom of the press, and make a note of your arguments for and against. How do you think the press should be controlled, if at all?

In your groups, brainstorm a few examples of political regimes which have stifled the press. Why did/do they do it?

P | I | U· **Newspaper survey**

► In small groups, write a list of ten questions about the newspaper reading habits of the rest of the class, e.g. *Do you read a newspaper every day? Which part do you read first?*

Work with a partner from another group and ask each other your questions.

Take turns to come to the board and write up your two most interesting questions. Choose one each and survey the class, then report back, e.g. *Twenty-five per cent of the students in the class read the Sunday papers.*

► In pairs, brainstorm ten things that a newspaper can be used for, apart from reading it, *e.g. a flyswatter.* Compare your list with another pair.

P | I | U· **Projects**

► Find two articles from different newspapers about the same story and bring them into class. In groups, make notes about the differences in how the story is covered.

► We're going to create a students' rag – a newspaper by the students, for the students. In pairs, brainstorm some sections of a daily paper.

> leader, horoscope, home news, obituaries, overseas news, situations vacant, listings, fashion, games page, TV and radio, gossip, sport, comment and analysis

Choose a section to work on in your own time. (Invite students to form small groups if they wish.) Your articles can be about other students in class, or the teachers. Look for some magazine photos to use, too. In a few weeks we will all put our work together. (You'll need glue and scissors for this part. If the students have the IT skills, they can compile the paper on computer.)

► Look in the press and find an advertisement you like and one you don't. In the next lesson, work in small groups and explain why you like or dislike them. Try to identify the persuasive techniques used by advertisers. As a group, choose your favourite advert.

## Politics

E P I U+ **Parliamentary questions**

▶ In groups of three or four, discuss the differences between these systems of government: democracy, communism, fascism, benevolent dictatorship.

▶ Work in groups. Answer these questions about UK politics.

> What are the main political parties in the UK? (Labour, Liberal Democrats, Conservative)
> What are the two Houses of Parliament? (Commons, Lords)
> Who is the current Prime Minister of the UK?
> Who are the leaders of the opposition?
> What does MP stand for? (Member of Parliament)
> How many MPs are there in the UK? (659)
> How often are there elections for parliament? (Every five years, at the longest)
> What is the Palace of Westminster? (Houses of Parliament)
> When did women get the vote? (1918)
> Where does the Prime Minister live? (10 Downing Street)
> What's the name of the clock tower in Westminster Palace? (Big Ben – actually the name of the bell)
> Can you name one of the more radical parties in the UK? (British National Party, Socialist Worker's Party)
> Can you name a famous Prime Minister from the past? (Churchill, Thatcher, etc.)
> What does 'Tory' mean? (Conservative)

(Variation: Ask these questions about US politics.)

> What are the main political parties in the USA? (Republican, Democrat)
> What are the two Houses of Congress? (Senate, House of Representatives)
> Who is the current President of the USA?
> How many Representatives/Senators are there? (435/100)
> How often are there elections for President/Representatives/Senators? (every 4/6/2 years)
> Where is the American government located? (Capitol Hill)
> Where does the president live? (The White House, 1600 Pennsylvania Avenue)
> When did women get the vote? (1869 – in Wyoming)
> How many former US presidents can you name?

(Single nationality classes.) Write a similar set of questions about your own parliamentary system to test the other groups. Swap questions with another group to answer.

(Mixed nationality classes.) Tell each other about the political system in your country.

E P I U+ **Frontiers** ⚠

Work in small groups and write a short definition of a country. Try to include as many of these factors as you can.

> language, geography, ethnic minorities, regional autonomy, religion, history, colonialism

Give some examples of groups who are fighting for their independence, e.g. the Kurds in Iraq, the Tibetans in China. Which of these factors are relevant to their arguments? What methods do they use to achieve their aims? What do you think of their struggle? What do you think is the best solution to each problem?

What would happen if there were no frontiers?

E P I U-

## Debate ⚠

Here is a motion for a debate: There's nothing wrong with stealing from the rich to give to the poor.

Work in two groups: those for the motion and those against. (Place undecided students in the smaller group. One student could chair the debate.)

Brainstorm your arguments, and anticipate the arguments of the other side. Choose three people to represent the group. Conduct the debate, following this sequence.

1 Group A, present your arguments for the motion.
Group B, present your arguments against the motion.
2 Group A, support your arguments and criticise Group B's arguments.
Group B, support your arguments and criticise Group A's arguments.
3 Group A, sum up.
Group B, sum up.
4 Take a class vote.

(With large classes, run two debates at opposite ends of the room. Here are some alternative topics. Write up a contentious statement as a motion.)

> censorship of the press, military service, blood sports, GM food, euthanasia, the welfare state, zoos, cloning, terrorism, globalisation, drugs, environment

P I U-

## Good and bad

Work in two teams, A and B. When I call out the topic, someone from team A must quickly give an advantage. Then someone from team B must quickly give a disadvantage, beginning with 'Yes, but ...'.

> TV, cars, soap, clothes, death, alcohol, the monarchy, coffee, having a baby, the welfare state, freedom, being self-employed, cats and dogs, English as a world language, hitchhiking, living in the UK, computers, being a man, being a woman

(Variation: Alternate which team gives the advantage and disadvantage.)

P I U-

## Sort it out

Work in small groups. Imagine you live together and that there are lots of problems in the house. When I tell you the problem, you should discuss it and agree what to do. However, one of you is being obstructive; whatever the others agree to do, you oppose. (Choose one student in each group to play this role.)

| | |
|---|---|
| the spiders in the bath | the neighbours' parties |
| the mice in the kitchen | the dog hairs on the sofa |
| the smelly old carpet | all the dirty dishes |
| the broken window | the overgrown garden |

P I U-

## Equal opportunities ⚠

What is a 'minority group' in society? Do you think minorities are treated fairly in your country? Can you think of any political figures who have fought for the rights of oppressed minorities?

In small groups, discuss and agree an equal opportunities policy for a large company. Choose a secretary to keep notes of your decisions. Include these issues.

> race, gender, disability, religion, sexual orientation, political opinion, language

**Left and right**

Shout out some areas of policy for a political party. (Write them on the board.)

> education, economy, environment, immigration, the national health system,
> international relations, transport, agriculture, education, crime, defence

Work in three groups: A, B and C.

Group A, you are a right-wing party. Agree your policy on the areas you brainstormed.
Group B, you are a left-wing party. Agree your policy on the areas you brainstormed.
Group C, you are TV journalists. Prepare some questions about each area of policy.

Work in groups of three, one each from groups A, B and C. Role-play a short TV debate about each area of policy.

E P I U+ **Projects** (www)

▶ Make notes about a major political story happening at the moment. Sources can include TV/radio news, newspapers, the Internet or conversations with other people who are interested in the same story. Compose a news report to read out to the class. If there are two of you interested in the same story, do it as newsreader and an on-the-spot reporter.

▶ Visit the White House website and make notes about what the US president is doing at the moment. Compare notes with a partner.

## Relationships

E P I U+ **Defining relationships**

▶ Listen to this message and discuss in pairs the relationships between the people in it.

> John, I've just gone out to get some pizza for the kids' dinner. They should be back from the park with Lisa soon. Don't touch the kitchen wall – the paint's still wet. Jean sent you an e-mail. Don't worry – I didn't read it! Oh, and if Chris calls, I'm not here tonight. Pat x

▶ Tell each other about some of the relationships you are in, e.g. *husband/wife, student/teacher, tenant/landlord, daughter/father,* etc.

▶ In pairs, choose two or three of the following sentences and spend a few minutes discussing the events that led to the person saying them.

> I'm in love!   We've split up!   I'll never speak to them again!   I've left my job!

Swap partners with another pair. Student A, say a sentence. Student B, ask as many questions as you can to find out about the situation. Then swap roles.

E P I U+ **Life goes on**

In groups, discuss how someone's personal and/or professional relationships can be affected by these changes.

> winning the lottery, getting promoted at work, getting divorced,
> having a baby, relocating to a different town/country, alcoholism

Tell the rest of the group about any life-changing events that have happened to you, or somebody you know.

## Friendship

► In pairs, tell each other about your best friend at school, and your best friend now. Is it the same person? Can men and women be best friends?

► Discuss these sayings. Do you agree with them?

> Love me, love my dog.
> Opposites attract.
> A friend in need is a friend indeed.
> Absence makes the heart grow fonder.
> When poverty comes in through the door, love flies out the window.
> Blood is thicker than water.

Do you have any similar sayings in your country? Tell us a few of them.

## Love  ⚠

Do you believe in love at first sight? Does anyone know the story of Romeo and Juliet? (Elicit the story, one sentence at a time from those who know it, with a question about each line from those who don't, e.g. *They met at a party. Whose party was it?*)

In small groups, discuss the way relationships begin in different cultures. What are the most important foundations of a successful relationship? Compare your ideas with another group.

## Famous couples

Here are some people from famous relationships. When you hear the names, shout out their partners and tell us something about the relationship.

> Samson, Bonnie, John Lennon, Princess Diana, Posh Spice, Napoleon, Anthony, Romeo

(If the class is mixed nationality.) In small groups, tell each other about a famous couple from your own country.

## Lonely Hearts  ⚠

► In pairs, write two short announcements for a lonely hearts section in a magazine. They should not be for yourselves, but for an imaginary man and woman. Here are two examples.

> **Jill of all Trades:** spontaneous, energetic F, 31, into climbing, sailing, tennis, dancing, drumming. Seeks honest straightforward M with GSOH for friendship+. PO Box 11483.
>
> **Tolerant, Sensitive,** considerate M, 29, journalist, likes socialising, music, film. WLTM creative sensitive F 25–35. PO Box 12951.

Take one announcement each and mingle with the rest of the class to see if there's another lonely heart who is compatible with yours. You must find a partner, so you may have to settle for someone who is 'not incompatible'. Talk with your new partner and discuss how you think the relationship is going to develop.

► In groups, discuss the following questions.

> Why do people join dating agencies? Do such relationships work out?
> What other ways are there of finding romance?
> What is a 'blind date'?
> Do you think it's possible to meet your future husband/wife on the Internet?

**Marriage** ⚠

► In pairs, discuss your opinions on these aspects of marriage.

> the best age to get married
> the importance of religion to marriage
> the advantages and disadvantages of arranged marriages

Discuss the most common reasons for getting married and getting divorced.

► In pairs, agree the terms of a marriage contract to make the responsibilities of each person clear. Here are some issues to consider.

> relationships with other people, looking after babies, paying the bills, housework, making money, spending money, hours spent at work and at home, honesty

 **Family**

► What are the differences between nuclear families and extended families? (Elicit comparisons from the class, e.g. *Grandparents are not as well looked after by nuclear families.*)

In pairs, compare your families when you were children. Use these questions to help you.

> How many people were there?     Who was the head of the family?
> Did you get on with everyone?     How often did you see your cousins?
> Were your parents strict?     Did you have any pets?

► In small groups, discuss these questions.

> How has family life changed during your lifetime?
> Do you think it's acceptable for parents to smack children?
> Should grandparents be put in old people's homes?
> Is it acceptable to have more than one husband or wife?
> What are the advantages and disadvantages of being a single parent?

 **Project**

Find a lonely hearts section in a magazine and bring it into class. Can you see any two people in the section who might be compatible?

## Science and technology

**Discoveries and inventions**

What technological developments and scientific discoveries have there been in the last hundred years?

In small groups, brainstorm discoveries/inventions and the advances that have resulted from them. Agree on a list of the top ten most significant discoveries and inventions. Here are some suggestions.

> the wheel, electricity, the light bulb, vaccinations, nuclear fission,
> the silicon chip, the internal combustion engine, printing, the alphabet

What would happen if there was suddenly no electricity in the world?

## Science fact or fiction?

Has anybody in the class read a good science fiction book, e.g. *Brave New World* or *Fahrenheit 451*? Tell us about the kind of future society depicted in the book you read. Has any of it already come true?

In small groups, discuss the ways technology can help society in the future, and the ways it can also threaten society.

## Alternative science ⚠

In groups, discuss the evidence for these phenomena, and your opinions about them.

ESP (extra sensory perception), palmistry, life after death, UFOs, astrology, holistic medicine

## Information technology

► What are the greatest changes brought about by computers? Do you think there will ever be intelligent computers, i.e. computers that can learn?

In groups, list the advantages and disadvantages of modern technologies, e.g. *International telephone calls are very cheap. Working on computers all day is bad for your health.*

► In groups, imagine a world without computers. How would it affect your day-to-day life? Make a list of five inconveniences, e.g. *I'd have to go to the library to get information rather than look on the Internet.*

## Project  (www)

Use the Internet to find out about one of these people and their contribution to science. In the next lesson, exchange information with another student.

Guglielmo Marconi, Charles Babbage, Marie Curie, Elisha Otis, Louis Pasteur, William Caxton, Thomas Edison, Jean Foucault, Enrico Fermi, Albert Einstein

## Sport

## Sports talk

In small groups, make top-ten lists for these categories.

sportspeople, sporting nations, events in sport, sporting disasters

Compare your lists with another group.

## Sporting extremes

► What extreme sports can you think of? (Elicit as many as possible and write them on the board.) Has anyone done any of them? Tell us about it.

skydiving, snowboarding, bungee jumping, mountain biking, surfing, paragliding

► In groups, imagine you have just won a major international competition in your sport. Write a script for a television interview. Choose two of you to read it out to the class.

► In groups, invent a new sport, e.g. *It's played with a bean bag and a sock. The contestants are blindfolded ... .* Which group's sport do you think should be included in the next Olympic Games?

**Guess the game**

In pairs, take turns to think of a sport for your partner to guess. You can ask twenty questions and your partner can only answer 'yes' or 'no'.

(With mixed nationality classes, find out how many of them know one of their national sports, e.g. sumo wrestling, boules, cricket, kabbadi, baseball, ice hockey. Put them into groups with students who do not know the sport so that they can explain it to them.)

**Blood sports** ⚠

What different blood sports can you think of? Do you think there is anything wrong with killing animals for sport?

Work in two groups, those who support blood sports, and those who are against. Prepare as many arguments in support of your position as you can. Try to predict the arguments of the other group.

Work with a partner from the other group. Compare your arguments. Can your partner manage to persuade you to change your position?

**Project** (www)

Use the Internet to research your favourite sportsperson. Prepare a brief presentation for the next lesson.

## Stories

**Reading habits**

► How important is storytelling in your culture? Do you think it is important to tell young children stories? Why (not)? Find out about your partner's reading habits. Here are some questions to help you.

> Are you reading a book in your free time? What's it about?
> What kind of books do you usually read? Why?
> What's the best book you've ever read? Why did you like it so much?
> Are you a fast reader?
> Do you read magazines or comics? Which ones?
> What do you think of e-books? Will they ever replace traditional books?

► Estimate how much time you spend reading every day and how much time you spend watching TV. Note the times down on a piece of paper. Below that draw a pie chart including the following kinds of reading.

> novels, 'quality' newspapers/magazines, other press/comics, signs/hoardings, instructions, study books, computer screens

Mingle with the rest of the class and compare your notes and pie chart with other students.

**Planning a story**

In small groups, make notes on the location, character and first scene for these types of story

> romance, horror, adventure, whodunnit, fairy tale

Choose your favourite and agree how the story develops and ends.

## Genres

What different types of story can you think of? (Write suggestions on the board as a list.)

> western, disaster, historical, gangster story, love story, war, detective, family saga, sci-fi

Can you think of any examples for each type? Who wrote them?

Work in small groups. Each group is going to write the beginning of a story. I'll tell you which type. (Allocate a different type to each group.) Appoint a secretary to do the writing, on a separate piece of paper with your names at the top. (Give the groups a few minutes to begin their stories.)

Now pass your story to the next group, and continue the story you receive. (Repeat this two or three times, and then pass the stories back to the groups that started them.)

Correct any mistakes you find in the other groups' writing, and choose a volunteer to read the story to the class.

## Fortunately, unfortunately

Work in two groups, A and B. You are going to continue some stories. Group A, you want a happy ending. Group B, you want a sad ending. Continue these story beginnings starting with 'fortunately' if you are in Group A, and 'unfortunately' if you are in Group B.

(The two groups take it in turns to add to the story.)

> He stepped down from the train and there she was on the platform ...
> Frank's car suddenly broke down in the middle of the forest. It was a dark night ...
> The prince was riding through the valley on his horse ...
> We were just a poor family when they discovered oil on our land ...

(After four or five additions, tell the next group to finish the story. Another way to do this is for pairs of students to write their addition to the story, fold the paper so that only their line is visible and then pass it on to the next pair, who repeat the process.)

## Guided story telling

Work in groups of four. Here's the beginning of a story. (Write it on the board.)

> There was an old lady living in a cottage in the forest with her granddaughter ...

Student A, describe the old lady to the rest of the group.
Student B, describe the granddaughter.
Student C, describe the cottage.
Student D, describe the forest and beyond.

(Write up the next line.)

> One day a young man knocked at the door ...

Agree a description of the young man: who he was, where he was from, why he was calling at the house, etc. Finish the story, taking turns to add one sentence each. When you have finished, work with a partner from another group and tell each other your finished story.

## Story words

In groups, select twenty recently learnt items of vocabulary and write them on a large piece of paper. Swap your paper with another group. Put the one you receive in the middle of your group and take turns to use the words in a story, adding one line each.

**Comprehension questions**

Look at the comprehension questions and tell me what you think the story is about. What's going to happen next?

> Why did Henry kill Roderick? Who did he call then? Were the diamonds still there? How did Henry get away? Why did Fiona shout, 'You don't need the gun, Jack'?

In small groups, write ten similar questions for a another story which another group is going to write. Swap your list of questions with another group, and write the story for the questions you receive.

**Once upon a time**

▶ (Find out how many folk stories the students know and put them into two or three groups in which they all know the same story. Here are some possible stories.)

> Sleeping Beauty, Hansel and Grettel, Snow White and the Seven Dwarves, Jack and the Beanstalk, Dracula, Goldilocks, The Ugly Duckling

(In their groups, students discuss the story and remind each other of how it goes, then tell the story to the class, taking turns to say one line each.)

▶ (With mixed nationality classes, ask the students to think of a folk story from their countries. Put them in groups with one or two students telling their stories to the others, or get one volunteer to tell the story to the whole class.)

**Mini sagas**

I'm going to dictate the story of Romeo and Juliet. Write it down.

> Romeo and Juliet fell deeply in love, but their parents did not get on. Everything became tragic when Juliet's cousin killed Romeo's best friend. There was a misunderstanding about a sleeping potion. Romeo, thinking Juliet was dead, committed suicide. Juliet awoke, saw Romeo, made a speech, and killed herself too.

How many words are there in the story? There should be fifty.

In pairs, write another well-known story, or the summary of a film, in exactly fifty words. Swap stories with another pair. Have they missed anything important? If so, try to add it without increasing the total number of words.

**Picture story**

In four groups, choose one person to draw four pictures on separate pieces of paper: 1) an animate object, 2) an inanimate object, 3) a place, 4) an action. (Collect them all together and shuffle them.) Join another group so that there are two groups. Take half the pictures each and use all the pictures your group receives to compose a story.

**Projects** (www)

▶ (For mixed nationality classes). Look up a folk story from your country on the Internet. Ideally, it should contain illustrations and be no longer than two sides of A4 when printed out. Bring your story to class and put it up on the wall for the others to read.

▶ Look up urban legends on the Internet and print one of them out to bring to the next lesson. In class, decide which one is the most interesting and which is the most unbelievable.

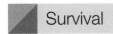

## Survival

**Message in a bottle**

Does anyone know the story of Robinson Crusoe or the film *Castaway*? (Elicit some of the details.) In small groups, imagine you have been shipwrecked on a desert island. Choose ten objects to save from the ship and explain why you chose them. Compare your list with another group.

(On the board, draw a picture of a floating bottle with a rolled up message in it.) What is in the bottle? It tells the story of someone's shipwreck on a desert island and consequent struggle for survival. In your groups, talk together and make notes about what is contained in the message and when it was sent, e.g. *Left London June 1757. Violent storm, South Pacific. No survivors, just me and cat. Found coconuts ...*

When you have finished, choose someone from your group to read out your message. As a whole class, decide which of the castaways you think most deserves to be rescued.

In the same groups, discuss what you know about the day-to-day life on board a large sailing boat of that time. Talk about the following.

> duties, food, dangers, punishments, warfare, equipment, weapons

**Alive!**

Imagine you are drifting on a raft in the middle of the ocean. How would you survive? (Elicit as many of these issues as possible.)

> moving the raft, navigation, protection from the sun, signals, food, water, morale

In three groups, imagine you are the survivors of a plane crash. The aircraft cannot be repaired but it did not catch fire. You don't know where the nearest people are. One of you has a broken leg. Agree the best plan for survival and make notes. I'm going to tell you what type of environment you find yourselves in.

> 1 The middle of the desert   2 The Amazon jungle   3 The arctic

Pass your plan to the next group. Can you spot any problems with their plan? Ask questions to check the details, and tell them where you think they went wrong.

**The great escape**   ⚠

In two groups, design a regime for a high-security prison that no one will be able to escape from. Include a plan of the building, times the different activities happen (exercise time, lights out, etc.) and the visiting rights of the prisoners. Exchange plans with another group and work out how to escape from their prison.

Work with a partner from the other group. Sit opposite each other across the table.

Student A, you are visiting Student B in prison. You are going to help him/her to escape. Student B, tell Student A about your escape plans and arrange for the help you will need when you are outside the prison walls.

Then swap roles.

**Project**   (www)

Look up wilderness survival skills on the Internet. Make notes about one of the survival tips you see. In the next lesson, get into groups and share what you have learnt.

In the same groups, discuss how you would survive for a year in the wilderness.

## Television

E P I U+ **Prime time**

► (Ask the class which English language programmes are shown in their country. Are they dubbed or given subtitles? Elicit the following programmes by giving clues, e.g. *It's about a silly man who doesn't talk properly and keeps making mistakes.*)

> Mr Bean, Friends, Star Trek, The Simpsons, The X Files, ER, Sesame Street, Who wants to be a Millionaire? Blind Date, Big Brother, Crime Scene Investigation

If you know one of these programmes, describe it to another student who has never seen it.

► In groups, brainstorm a list of ten different kinds of programme and then work on your own to put the list in order from your most to least favourite. Compare your order with the rest of the group. (Elicit the genres and write them on the board. Here are some possibilities.)

> current affairs, nature/wildlife, soap operas, sport, history, music, cookery, comedy, police dramas, travel, talk shows, quizzes, weather forecast, DIY/gardening

E P I U+ **Survey**

I'm going to dictate one question to each person. Mingle and ask all the other students your question. Make a note of their answers.

> Is there more than one TV in your home?
> Would you like to live without a TV?
> How many hours a week do you watch TV?
> Do you watch soap operas? Which ones?
> How often do you watch English language programmes?
> Do you watch sport? Which ones?
> What is your favourite TV programme?
> Do you watch nature programmes?
> Is there too much violence on TV?
> Do you leave the TV on when you're not watching it?
> Should advertisements aimed at children be banned?
> Do you watch the news every day?

Take turns to read out your question and the result of your survey, e.g. *I asked the class if there was more than one TV in their house. Two of them said there was – that's 20 per cent. One student had a TV in every room.*

E P I U+ **TV adverts**

What are your favourite TV advertisements? Do you think you are influenced by TV advertising? Why (not)?

In small groups, imagine you work for an advertising agency. Design a TV advertisement for one of these products.

> a new shampoo, an economical car, a glamorous perfume, a strong beer, a healthy margarine, fashionable jeans, an anti-ageing cream, a lawnmower

Imagine the rest of the class are your clients. Describe your advertising campaign and try to persuade them to commission it.

P | I | U+ **Projects**

▶ Watch the news on TV tonight and make notes about the stories, sport and weather forecast. Turn them into headlines. In groups, compare your headlines. How similar are they?

▶ Bring in a TV guide for the evening of the next lesson. In small groups, try to agree on an evening's viewing. You can only watch one TV and you can't record anything.

## Time

P | I | U+ **Time keepers**

In groups, discuss these questions.

> Who's the most punctual student in the class?
> How many students in your group use a calendar? What for?
> How many of you have got a watch? How often do you look at it?
> What is your favourite time of day/year?
> Name something that is a waste of time.
> What is 'quality time'? What is the 'leisure society'?

P | I | U+ **Time flies**

In small groups, discuss and explain these sayings. Do you agree or disagree with them?

> Time is a great healer. Time is money. Time waits for no one. Tomorrow never comes. Time flies when you're having fun. There's no time like the present. You're only young once. You cannot save time; you can only spend it.

P | I | U+ **Teacher's time**

In pairs, write three questions to ask me about how I spend my time. I'll answer any correctly formed questions honestly. Use these expressions.

> How long does it take you to ...?
> How much time do you spend ...?
> How many times a day/week/year do you ...?

Use the same kinds of question to find out about your partner.

P | I | U+ **Lifetime**

▶ In small groups, discuss when the best time in life is to do these things.

> get married, retire, have kids, travel, leave home

▶ In small groups, put these words in chronological order.

> homework, nappies, retirement, exams, housework, marriage, parties, acne, responsibility, paper aeroplanes, grey hair, teddy bears

▶ Draw a graph of your own life, with the line rising for good periods and falling for bad ones. In pairs, explain the features of your graphs to each other.

## Transport

**Transport links**

▶ What's the most unusual form of transport you have ever used?

In small groups, brainstorm as many kinds of transport as you can, and think of a few phrases to describe them, e.g. *bicycle – cheap, uncomfortable in bad weather, dangerous in heavy traffic, no pollution.*

Rank the types of transport according to a criterion of your choosing e.g. speed, size, environmental friendliness, etc. Read out your list. Can the others guess the criterion?

▶ In small groups, discuss the words and ideas you associate with the following kinds of transport, e.g. submarine – *secrecy, The Cold War, Kursk.*

> gondola, tank, hot-air balloon, helicopter, yacht, bicycle, horse and carriage, Rolls-Royce, hang glider, mule, double-decker bus, elephant, spaceship

Tell each other about any of the forms of transport you have used and any that you'd really like to experience.

**Public transport**

How does the public transport system here compare with the system in another city you know well? How do you travel to class?

In small groups, discuss the advantages and disadvantages of cycling and driving to work.

Agree a list of ten transport policies for a smoggy, congested, over-populated city. You will need to find a way of encouraging people out of their cars and onto public transport.

**Journeys**

▶ In small groups, tell each other about your most recent journey to another country.

> how you planned it, how you travelled, what you saw and did on the way, what you expected to see when you arrived, your first impressions when you arrived, things that were difficult to get used to, where you stayed

▶ In pairs, write some questions that an immigration officer might ask someone at passport control. Use these words.

> Why? What? Who? Where? How long? Have you ever? When?

Swap partners with another pair and role-play the conversation.

Student A, you are a passenger at passport control.
Student B, you are an immigration officer

**Cars**

▶ On a piece of paper, make some notes about the model and colour of car you would most like to own, but don't write your name. I'll collect them and read them out. Try to guess who wants each car.

▶ Who has a driving licence? How many lessons did you have? Did you pass first time? Tell us about what happened during your driving test.

In small groups, discuss the differences between the highway code in the UK/USA and in your country.

▶ In small groups, tell each other about a memorable car journey.

**Project**

Look up some car hire companies on the Internet. Find the cheapest rate for a week's hire, but be careful to check the mileage allowance, the deposit, the insurance excess, etc. Compare your research with a partner.

# Work

**The job market**

Do people spend too much of their lives working? What is the employment situation like in your country? What are the effects of globalisation on the job market?

In small groups, tell each other about these jobs.

> 1  the best / worst / most interesting / most dangerous job you have done
> 2  the best / worst / most interesting / most dangerous job in the world

**Job description** ⚠

Here are some important aspects of a job.

> duties, pay, the boss, benefits, training, holidays, health and safety, promotion, hours of work, experience, overtime, unions, job security

Ask me questions about these aspects of my job. (Pretend only to hear the grammatically correct questions.)

In pairs, use similar questions to interview your partner about his/her job. (If fewer than half the students are in work, put them in small groups. If no one is working, ask them to imagine a job they would like.)

**Globalisation**

Work in two groups of six. (If the class does not divide, make one or more groups smaller and take away one of the roles below.) Each of you choose a different number from 1 to 6. You are going to discuss the building of a clothes factory in a poor country. I'm going to give you a role according to the number you chose.

In the rich country:
1  Businessman/investor
2  Anti-capitalist protestor
3  Factory worker

In the poor country:
4  Unemployed factory worker
5  Politician
6  Environmentalist

Take turns to say if you are in favour of the factory and how it will affect your life and the country if it is built. Assuming that the factory is going ahead, talk together as a group to negotiate the best possible deal for everybody concerned.

# Functions

## Ability

E P I U+ **Present ability**

▶ Mingle and find out whether the other students in the class can or cannot do these things. Keep a note of their answers for a feedback session.

> speak French, swim, drive, paint, juggle, play chess, ride a horse, go cross-eyed, cook well, sing well, knit, wiggle their ears, do handstands, do the splits

▶ Write a list of things that you cannot do, but which you think other students in class can do. Take turns to read some of them out and see if they are true, e.g. *I can't swim, but I think Elena can.*

E P I U+ **Something special**

▶ What things can Superman do? Do you know anybody with lots of abilities? Who is it and what can he/she do?

In groups of three or four, find out what special abilities you've got between you. Here are some topics to think about. Which group has got the most special abilities?

> cooking, sport, arts and crafts, science, professional skills, music

▶ In pairs, make a list of special abilities that animals have, e.g. *Bats can find things by echo location.*

Discuss how your life would change if you could do the same things.

E P I U+ **Past and future ability**

▶ In pairs, make a list of things people couldn't do one hundred years ago that they can do now, e.g. *People couldn't travel by plane.*

In pairs, make a list of things you can do now that you couldn't do when you were a child, and things you can't do now that you could do when you were a child, e.g. *When I was a child I could get up in the mornings really fast. I couldn't drive a car.*

In pairs, make a list of things that people will be able to do in the future that they cannot do now, e.g. *I think they'll be able to commute by air taxi.*

▶ Finish each sentence, once using *could* and once with *managed to*, e.g. *The car broke down, but we 1) could see a garage up the road. 2) managed to push it to a garage.*

> Despite losing my key, I ...      Although I was exhausted, ...
> I didn't have a life jacket, but I ...      I couldn't cook, but I ...

In pairs, read out the beginnings of the sentences and see if you can guess what your partner was able to do next.

In the same pairs, write the sentences again, but continue each one with *and + couldn't*, e.g. *The car broke down and we couldn't get it started again.*

On your own, write a sentence describing a small problem that you have had recently and how you managed to sort it out. Read out the beginning of the sentence for the rest of the class to guess what you did next.

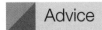

## Advice

### What you should do is ...

► In small groups, take turns to give each other advice for these situations using *should* and *ought to*, e.g. A – *My car doesn't start.* B – *You should check the battery.* C – *You ought to get a new one.*

> I'm bored. My husband/wife snores. My boss shouts at me. The roof is leaking.
> I'm going skiing. I feel very tired these days. I want to learn to speak Arabic.
> I'm losing a lot of weight. The neighbours are always arguing. I want to get fit.

► In small groups, agree the best way to continue these tips, and write your ideas down. Swap them with another group, and see if you agree with their advice.

> To look after your heart you should (not) ...
> To be happy in life you should (not) ...
> To learn a language you should (not) ...
> To drive safely you should (not) ...
> To bring up children well you should (not) ...
> To get on well with people you should (not) ...

► Work on your own. Write about a time you helped somebody by giving them some good advice. Then tell a partner about the problem and see if he/she would have given the same advice.

### Emergencies

In pairs, agree what you should do if someone ...

> is choking, has a fit, is burnt, has hypothermia, goes into labour, stops breathing, has swallowed something poisonous, has been electrocuted, has been bitten by a snake

### Agony aunts

Work in small groups. I'll give each group a problem. Write a letter to an agony aunt, giving details and asking for advice.

Group A, you are a wife with husband problems.
Group B, you are a husband with wife problems.
Group C, you are parents with adolescent child problems.

Here are some possible factors to consider.

> depression, alcoholism, unemployment, drugs, unfaithfulness, mortgage, pregnancy, nagging, TV, telephone, money, untidiness, friends, possessiveness

When you've finished your letter, pass it to another group. Write a reply to the letter you receive, giving advice about how to solve the problems. Then return the letter and your reply to the original group.

What do you think of the advice you have received? (Invite groups to read out the letters and replies.)

(Extension: Ask the students to work in groups of three – a husband, a wife and an adolescent child from the same family. Ask them to imagine that their family life is suffering because of the factors above. They are meeting to agree on some rules for making each other's lives more bearable.)

**Help!**

Imagine I have these problems. In groups of three, discuss each one and give me a piece of advice beginning *If I were you ...* . I'll give a point to the group whose advice I think is best, e.g. T – *I get awful headaches.* S – *If I were you, I'd go to the doctor.*

| | |
|---|---|
| I can never find my keys. | I'm overdrawn. |
| My son is terribly shy. | My mother nags me. |
| The garden is full of weeds. | There's too much to do at work. |
| People don't listen to me. | I haven't got any friends. |
| I can't stop hiccupping. | My parents are terribly strict. |
| I can't find a job. | My life is boring. |
| My neighbours keep fighting. | My mobile phone bill is huge. |

**Doctor, doctor!**

► In pairs, agree the best advice for someone with these symptoms.

| | | |
|---|---|---|
| I feel tired all the time. | I can't get to sleep. | I've got a sore throat. |
| I've got a bad cough. | I've got a high temperature. | My chest hurts. |

In pairs, write a list of other symptoms, making sure you both have a copy. Swap partners with another pair. Tell each other your symptoms and give a diagnosis and some advice.

► Write some advice from a doctor to a patient leaving hospital using these words.

bed, TV, food, work, exercise, medicine, injections, alcohol

In pairs, role-play a conversation between the doctor and patient, taking turns to be the doctor. After each piece of advice, try to find a way to avoid accepting it, e.g. D – *You should stay in bed for three days.* P – *But I have to go to work or the office will fall apart.* D – *Well, it's very important that you get some rest.*

**Proverbs**

In pairs, discuss the meaning of these proverbs.

A bird in the hand is worth two in the bush.
Make hay while the sun shines.
You can't judge a book by its cover
Too many cooks spoil the broth.
All that glitters is not gold.
Every cloud has a silver lining.
Don't throw the baby out with the bath water.
It's no use crying over spilt milk.

For each proverb, write a sentence expressing its meaning using *should / ought to*, e.g. *A bird in the hand is worth two in the bush. You should be content with what you have and not always look for more.*

Tell the class some proverbs from your language.

**Bad habits**

In two groups, brainstorm a list of adjectives to describe someone who is unbearable to live with. Write a piece of advice next to each one, e.g. *Lazy – You should tidy up the kitchen more.*

Take turns to read your advice to the other group and see if they can guess the adjectives.

## Past mistakes

▶ Work in pairs. I'm going to give each pair a different sentence describing a bad situation. Agree on a sequence of five mistakes that led up to the situation, and write it down. Swap your list with another pair. Read their sequence and discuss what the person should or shouldn't have done at each stage. Write a note of your advice and give it to the pair.

> Kevin was given a five-year prison sentence.
> The holiday was a complete disaster.
> They got divorced as soon as they could.
> Jack is living on the street now.
> The house is a complete ruin now.
> Sharon was given the sack.
> John went on to become a street sweeper.
> He had to take time off work due to nervous exhaustion.

▶ In groups, discuss these events, saying what people should have done to avoid them.

> the Titanic, the colonisation of America, World War II, Vietnam,
> an important event in your country, a current situation in the news

## Regrets

Work on your own and think about something you did that you wish you hadn't done or that you had done differently. Write a sentence about your regrets, e.g. *I should never have / I wish I hadn't jumped off that roof when I was playing with my friends.*

Work in small groups and take turns to read out your sentences and answer further questions, e.g. A – *Why did you jump off the roof?* B – *Oh, it was a dare.* A – *Did you break anything?* B – *Yes, I broke my ankle.*

## Buying and selling

## Products

Imagine you are buying some things in a street market. Look at this conversation.

> A – Good morning.
> B – Good morning. A kilo of onions, please.
> A – There you go. Anything else?
> B – Yes. I'll have a large beetroot.
> A – One large beetroot. Anything else?
> B – That's all, thanks.
> A – OK. That'll be €1 please.
> B – Here you are. Thanks.
> A – Bye.

In pairs, choose one of these shops and write a list of the things you sell. Write a few items to buy from each of the other shops. One of you will go shopping and the other will stay to mind the shop. Have conversations like the one on the board in each shop.

> chemist, market stall, newsagent, butcher, bakery,
> computer shop, post office, DIY shop, sports shop

E P I U+ **Money**

Ask each other questions about the things you have with you in class, using *buy, pay, spend* and *cost*. Follow this sequence and then make an offer for the thing in question.

> How much did you buy your pen for? I bought my pen for €3.
> How much did you pay for your pen? I paid €3 for my pen.
> How much did you spend on your pen? I spent €3 on my pen.
> How much did your pen cost? My pen cost €3.
> I'll give you €2 for it.

E P I U+ **Small ads**

Have you ever bought anything second-hand, advertised in a newspaper or on a notice board? What was it? Was it a bargain?

Work in pairs. (Designate alternate pairs A and B.)

Pair A, you are putting an advertisement in the local paper. The ad is 'House Clearance: everything must go.' Brainstorm ten items to include in the sale and give each a price, e.g. *cooker €50, racing bike €20*. Make sure you both make a copy of the list.

Pair B, you are trying to furnish a house as cheaply as possible. Write a list of ten items and a budget for each one. Make sure you both make a copy of the list.

Swap partners with another pair and role-play this telephone conversation.

Student A, try to sell all your items for the best price possible, even if they're not on Student B's list.

Student B, find out if the items you want are for sale. Get as much information as possible, and try to negotiate a better price.

 Complaining and criticising

E P I U+ **Shops**

Work in groups of three. I'm going to give you some different types of shop. When you hear the shop, quickly agree on a complaint, e.g. T – *Shoe shop.* S – *I bought these shoes yesterday and the heel's already broken.*

> garage, delicatessen, bakery, supermarket, photo developers,
> DIY shop, greengrocer, chemist, boutique, toy shop

(After you have read out the whole list, elicit some of the complaints.)

In your groups, choose your favourite complaint and role-play this conversation.

Student A, you are an argumentative customer.
Student B, you are an unhelpful shop assistant.
Student C, you are the manager, called to sort out the problem.

E P I U+ **For crying out loud**

In small groups, tell each other about a real complaint you have made. Did you express your misgivings in a polite but assertive way? Was your complaint properly dealt with?

Choose the most interesting complaint and write a script for it to read out to the class.

## Returns

P I U+

Imagine you are in a shop complaining to the sales assistant. In pairs, write a mini dialogue with the following pairs of words, e.g. Customer – *I asked for a size 12, but you gave me a size 14.* Assistant – *I'm terribly sorry, madam. I'll get you a size 14.*

> brown/black, satin/matt, lager/bitter, brown/white, a 10 Euro note / a 20 Euro note
> 2 five-kilo bags / 5 two-kilo bags, 3 amp/13 amp, hamburger/fishburger

Swap dialogues with another pair, and practise reading them.

## Flat share problems

P I U+

In pairs, imagine you are flatmates. Role-play a discussion and give each other advice about how to change your behaviour, e.g. A – *You shouldn't leave your bike in the hall, it makes it dirty.* B – *Why don't you relax more? It's easy to clean up later.*

Student A, you are very tidy, like peace and quiet, study hard, don't go out very much, usually pay the bills on time, do most of the cooking and housework.

Student B, you are very untidy, like loud music/TV, can't be bothered to study, like parties, are always broke, hate cooking and housework.

## Where am I?

P I U+

In pairs, listen to my complaints. After each one, write down where I am.

> 1 Typical! You wait half an hour and then three come along at once! (bus stop)
> 2 This venison is undercooked and the Jerusalem artichokes are mushy. (restaurant)
> 3 You said it was just a small problem with the choke, but you've charged me for a new carburettor and brake pads. (mechanic's garage)
> 4 We brought Granddad here for a hip replacement and you took out his appendix. (hospital)
> 5 Whenever I press the mute button, it changes channel. (TV shop)
> 6 I was assured that it was a female, but it ate my prize goldfish. What are you going to do about it? (aquarium)
> 7 How can you charge me line rental when I'm pay-as-you-go? (mobile phone shop)
> 8 Look! It was only Valentine's day yesterday and the petals have already fallen off! (flower shop)
> 9 These are all blurred and there's a yellow line running through the whole lot. I know it's not the camera that's to blame. (photograph developers)
> 10 Excuse me. I asked for this with lemon, but no ice. (bar)

In pairs, write two more complaints. Read them out for the rest of the class to guess where you are.

## Letters of complaint

P I U+

Look at the following information about poor products or services.

| Car €999 (used) | Holiday €600 | Jacket €200 | EFL School |
|---|---|---|---|
| Noisy brakes | Filthy hotel | Tear in armpit | 30 students/class |
| Leaking sunroof | No swimming pool | Buttons missing | Wrong level |
| Faulty indicator | Construction work | Lining missing | Rude staff |
| Backfiring | 12-hour delay | Stain | Cold classroom |

In pairs, choose one of them and write a letter of complaint. Swap letters with another pair and write a reply, e.g. *In your brochure you said the hotel had a swimming pool.*

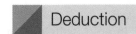

## Deduction

E P I U+ **Enigma**

Here is a five-letter word. (Write five blanks on the board.) Suggest some possible words. I'll write an X for every letter in your word that's the same as one of mine and in the right place. I'll write an O for every letter in your word that's the same as one of mine but in the wrong place. Try to deduce the correct letters, e.g.

| Suggestion | Code | Example deductions |
|---|---|---|
| P A P E R | OO | The word can't be *great* because there are only two letters the same. It could be *sport* or *teach*. |
| S P O R T | OO | There might be a 'p' and an 'r' in the word. |
| P R O V E | XX | The word can't include a 'p' or an 'o' otherwise there would an X for the 'p' in *paper* and for the 'o' in *sport*. |
| H O U S E | X | I think there's an 'e' at the end of the word. |
| P H O N E | X | There can't be an 'h' or an 'o', otherwise there would be an O for *house*. It can't be the 'n' in *phone* <u>and</u> the 's' in *house* so it must be the 'e' at the end. This means that the word can't have an 'a', 'u' or 'v'. The word must contain an 'r' and a 't'. It probably needs another vowel which will either be 'i' or 'e' because there isn't an 'a', 'o' or 'u'. |
| W R I T E | XXXXX | |

E P I U+ **Drawings**

I'm going to draw something on the board. After each line, try to guess what it is, e.g. *It might be a ... , It could be a ...* . (Draw these objects line by line, or invite a student to do it.)

> bicycle, house, washing machine, cat, toaster, toothbrush, man fishing

E P I U+ **Explanations**

► Work in pairs. I'll tell you about a situation. Discuss some possible explanations, e.g. T – *He isn't answering the phone.* S – *He might be in the shower. He must want us to leave him alone. Maybe the phone ringer is switched off.*

> The line is engaged. The fridge smells absolutely terrible. I'm working 16 hours a day at the moment. There's a lot of noise next door. Sheila is always smiling these days. They've decided not to publish my book. The baby is crying. The car won't start. He's wearing a Rolex. Carol's studying astrophysics.

► In pairs, make past deductions about these situations, e.g. T – *You've lost your bag.* S – *I must have left it on the bus. I can't have left it at home because I keep my bus pass in it.*

> Ray's got a lovely tan. The boss looks really tired. The hotel room was full of massive spiders. They didn't come to our wedding. I feel sick. Jess doesn't come to class any more. Charlie's got a black eye. They came back looking very disappointed. Suddenly they've got loads of money. My phone rang at three o'clock this morning.

## The next morning ⚠️

Imagine you have woken up on a Sunday morning with a terrible headache. You can't remember anything from the night before, but you discover some clues. Work in small groups and speculate about what happened.

> There's a strange telephone number with the letters CS in your pocket.
> There's a half-eaten hamburger in the kitchen, but you're a vegetarian.
> You've got a graze on your forehead.
> The front door is wide open.
> Nothing is missing from the flat.
> Your photo is on the front page of the morning paper.

## Classroom detectives

A body was discovered in the classroom during break and the police believe that someone in the class is the killer. (Reveal the information bit by bit, completing it as necessary.)

> There was a cigarette end next to the deceased's body, but he was a non-smoker.
> There was a suicide note, but it wasn't written in the deceased's handwriting.
> The note contained some grammar mistakes.
> Forensic evidence suggests that the killer had _____ hair.
> Forensic evidence suggests the killer was wearing something _____ (colour).

In small groups, identify the killer based on the information given to you, e.g. *It can't have been Anya because she's a non-smoker. It might have been Pedro because he's wearing a green jumper.*

## Lateral thinking

I'm going to give you a lateral thinking problem. (Write it on the board.)

> A man went to a party and drank some of the punch. He then left early. Everyone else at the party who drank the punch subsequently died of poisoning. Why?

In pairs, try to work out what happened, e.g. *He might have put the poison in the punch.*

(If no one gets it, give the students clues to lead them in the right direction. The answer is that the poison was in the ice cubes and the man had left the party before the ice cubes melted.)

(Here are some more lateral thinking problems that can be used for past deduction.)

> 1 A man is found dead in a field. He is clutching a broken match. What happened? (He and a number of other passengers were making a balloon trip in a desperate attempt to flee a country. The balloon had to lose weight to stop it from crashing. He drew the short match and had to jump.)
>
> 2 The music stopped. The circus tight-rope walker died. Explain. (She walked blindfolded over a high wire. The band played as she crossed and when the music stopped, it was the signal that she had reached the end of the wire and could safely alight. One day the conductor was taken ill and the stand-in conductor ended the piece of music too early. She stepped off to her death.)
>
> 3 A hunter aimed his rifle carefully and fired. Seconds later, he realised his mistake. Minutes later, he was dead. What happened? (It was winter. He fired the rifle near a snowy cliff, which started an avalanche.)

## Tell me why

I'm going to say some deduction sentences. Give me evidence to support each sentence, e.g. They must be in love. – *They are smiling at each other so romantically.*

> He must have left in a hurry. It can't have been properly packed. We must have met before somewhere. There can't have been anyone at home. You must have cooked it at the wrong temperature. They can't have given us the right directions. The thief must have got in through the window. She can't have told him. There must have been a party here.

## Project ⚠

Bring some family photos into the next lesson. Work in groups. Swap photos with another group. Discuss who's who in the photos you receive, e.g. *This must be Jose's brother. That might be his mum, but she seems so young. This can't be his wife, surely.*

Join the other group and see if you were right, e.g. *We reckon this is your brother, José.*

## Describing

## People

► I'm going to dictate some words. Put them under three headings: Hair/Face, Build and Opinion.

> tall, straight, thin, handsome, short, long, blue, beautiful, blond, medium height, curly, pretty, nice, smart, wavy

► Write a short description of someone in the class, but don't write the person's name. I'll collect the descriptions and read them out for you to guess who it is. (Tell the students who to describe, ideally someone facing them, and make sure everyone is included.)

## Perfect aliens ⚠

► Work in two groups, A and B. Group A, agree the description of the perfect woman. Group B, agree the description of the perfect man. What do you think about the other group's description? Would you like to be that person?

► In small groups, design an alien – the weirder the better. Get someone in the group to draw it. Describe it to the rest of the class and see if they can draw it. Compare your picture with theirs. Which description/picture does the class like the most?

## Things

► You're going to describe some objects hidden in this bag. (Collect objects from the students and include a few of your own.)

Put your hand in the bag and feel an object. Describe it to the class, but don't tell them what it is, e.g. *It feels soft and furry. It's small and light.* They will try to guess. (After a few guesses, invite the student to remove the object and show it to the class.)

► In pairs, think of an object which you use every day. Your partner will try to guess what it is by asking yes/no questions about these aspects.

> size, material, texture, colour, cost, when you use it, where you use it

## Location

▶ What are the correct prepositions?

| |
|---|
| _____ the top/bottom, _____ the left/right, _____ the middle/corner |

Work in two teams to play noughts and crosses. Tell me where to put your mark, using the expressions on the board. Play again in groups of three, with one of you marking the noughts and crosses. No pointing!

▶ What are the names of these shapes? (Draw a square, a triangle and a circle. Then draw picture 1 on the board.) Listen to this description of the picture. (Describe picture 1, e.g. *There's a large square. Inside it there's a small square at the top on the left. There's a small circle at the bottom in the middle.*)

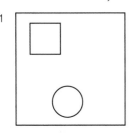 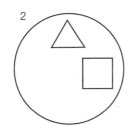 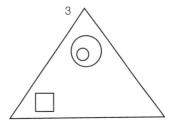

Write a similar description of these two pictures. (Draw pictures 2 and 3 on the board.) Compare your description with a partner.

▶ (Use pictures/realia to elicit oblong/rectangle, star, stripe and crescent.) In small groups, describe your national flag, or another flag you know well. What do the different colours and shapes represent?

I will describe some other national flags. In two teams, shout out the country each time to win a point.

## Gestures

How do people use their hands and faces in different countries to indicate these ideas?

| |
|---|
| You're mad.  Who cares?  I love you.  Delicious.  Hi.  Excellent.  I don't know. I'm angry.  Give it to me.  Pardon?  Not bad.  Disgusting.  OK.  Let's go. Goodbye.  Come here.  I don't understand.  Go away. (politely)  Go away. (rudely) |

## Mime

▶ I'm going to give each of you an imaginary object. You have to guess what it is from the way I pick it up and pass it to you. When you take it, say thank you and tell me what you're going to do with it. The rest of the class can suggest alternative uses.

| |
|---|
| brick, smelly sock, butterfly, bottle of wine, balloon, bunch of flowers, suitcase, snake |

▶ I'll give you the name of an object written on a piece of paper. Describe it using your hands only – showing its shape and size, and miming how you might use it. Another student will speak for you and say what it is, e.g. *It's about this big. It's square. It's got buttons like this. You can put things into it. It plays music ... A CD player!* If he/she is not right, shake your head and try again.

| |
|---|
| water melon, pocket calculator, camcorder, teddy bear, telephone directory, tricycle, freezer, toilet, public telephone box, water sprinkler, hairdryer, towel |

**Statues** ⚠

Stand in pairs facing each other. Strike a pose like a statue for the following. (Read these out one at a time. Only do this activity if all the students are outgoing.)

> boxer, explorer, general, angel, philosopher, dictator, hunter, supermodel, granny, hero

Work in groups of three. Students A and B, stand back to back. Student A, get into a really strange pose. Student C, tell Student B how to move in order to copy Student A's pose, like a mirror image.

**Same difference**

In pairs, describe to each other the differences between the members of these groups. You can look up any words you don't understand before you start your descriptions.

> 1 prawn, lobster, crab, shrimp
> 2 garlic, leek, onion, spring onion
> 3 tulip, rose, carnation, daffodil
> 4 beef, lamb, pork, venison
> 5 Spanish wine, Italian wine, French wine, German wine

Join another pair and tell each other which one you prefer from each group, and why.

**Wotsitsname?**

In pairs, role-play a conversation between a shopkeeper and a customer who has forgotten the name of the thing he/she wants. I'll give one student the name of an object and he/she has to describe it to the shopkeeper. The shopkeeper has to try to work out what it is, e.g. (A plug.) *Have you got one of those things that goes in the sink to stop the water from escaping?* (A good way to do this is to show the 'customer' the word in his/her own language, using a bilingual dictionary and hiding the English word.)

> teapot, cheese grater, paper clip, light bulb, ruler, rope, zip, mousetrap, mouse mat, corkscrew, scarf, thermos flask, compass, iron, colander, pin, rubber, stapler, whistle

**Favourite places**

In pairs, describe these places to your partner.

> your favourite room, your ideal house, your home town, your favourite place in the countryside/city

Choose one of them and write a description of it in 100–200 words.

**Haiku**

Does anybody know what a haiku is? Where are haiku from originally? How are they structured? (Traditionally, a haiku is a short poem describing a snapshot of the natural world and containing some reference to the season. They are from Japan, and have three lines. The first has five syllables, the second seven and the last five.) Look at these examples.

> underneath the bridge
> a Christmas tree abandoned
> in cold grey darkness
>
> a strand of cobweb
> drifting on the summer breeze
> catches the sunlight

In pairs, write two traditional haiku for different seasons. When you've finished, leave them on the table, then go around the classroom and read everybody else's.

## Directions

P I U+ **Place and movement**

Divide these words into two groups: place and direction. Some go in both.

> through, down, across, along, into, below, up, out,
> between, in, around, over, opposite, under, on, off

Choose any five that you are unsure of. Check them in a dictionary and write sentences with them. Compare your sentences with a partner.

P I U+ **My neighbourhood**

In pairs, find out who's got the best access to shops, amenities and transport links where they live, e.g. *There's a café on the corner of my street. Around the corner there's a post office. It's about a two minute walk to the nearest bus stop ...*

Copy this street plan. Tell me the names of the streets.

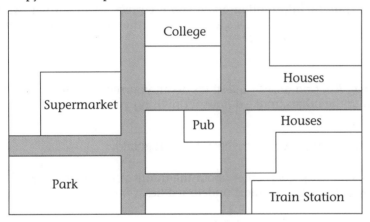

In pairs, decide where to put these places.

> bakery, car park, café, bus stop, newsagent, restaurant, chemist, corner shop

Form a group with another pair. Don't show them your map. Ask and answer questions about your maps to find any similarities.

P I U+ **Routes**

▶ In groups, discuss your journeys to school and find out whose is the most complicated. Choose a secretary for the group to write a description of the journey. Leave the description on your desk and look at the other groups' descriptions to find out who in the class has the worst journey.

▶ Imagine you have a job in the centre of a huge city and you have to choose where to live. In three groups, agree the advantages of your place and the disadvantages of the others. Group A, you have chosen the city centre. Group B, you have chosen the suburbs. Group C, you have chosen the countryside.

▶ Someone tell me exactly how to get from this classroom to the nearest café. (Choose a student to give directions, then see if anyone noticed anything missing.)

▶ In pairs, give each other directions from the airport to the place you live by public transport. Who has the most complicated journey, involving the most changes?

## Getting to know you

E P I U+ **Identity cards**

Copy this form. In pairs, ask and answer questions to fill in the form for your partner.

| | |
|---|---|
| Name | Three things I like |
| Age | |
| Languages spoken | Three things I don't like |
| Job | |
| Marital status | My ambition |
| Children | |

Swap forms and check that the information about you is correct. Swap partners with another pair and have a look at each other's forms. Ask further questions, e.g. *It says here that you like art. Who is your favourite artist?*

E P I U+ **Tell the truth**

Work in groups of three. Ask and answer questions about yourselves, but tell some lies as well. While you listen to the others, make a note of anything you think is a lie. Talk about these subjects.

> hobbies, job, house/flat, home town, family/friends, background

When you've finished, challenge each other about the things you think are lies. The winner is the person who included the most undetected lies.

E P I U+ **Introductions**

▶ Take turns to introduce yourselves and those who have already introduced themselves.
Student A, introduce yourself and say something you like.
Student B, introduce yourself, say something you like and introduce Student A.
Student C, introduce yourself, say something you like and introduce Students A and B.

If someone makes a mistake, the next student starts again. Continue like this until there's only one student left who has not made a mistake. That person is the winner.

▶ Introduce and describe yourself to the class, saying where you are from and what you like, but only using words that begin with the same letter as your name, e.g. *I'm marvellous Maria from Mexico and I like mountains and mice.*

E P I U+ **Guessing game** ⚠

In pairs, look at the pair sitting opposite you and make guesses about them using these ideas. Who do you think ...

> reads a lot of books? eats chocolate? likes babies? cooks a lot? is a bit shy?
> has a pet? is very tidy? likes dancing? is romantic? is a rebel? has lots of friends?
> works hard? is very creative? is very fit? plays a musical instrument?

When you have finished, join the other pair and check if your guesses were correct.

**Know how**

▶ Does anybody in the class know how to change a plug? (Elicit vocabulary through mime and a diagram of a plug on the board.)

In pairs, take turns to tell your partner how to do these things using *First, Then, After that* and *Finally*. While you listen to your partner's explanation, make a note on anything he/she misses.

> get the milk out of a coconut, make a cup of tea, print a Word document, mend a puncture, take a photograph, put up a shelf, look a word up in the dictionary, do a dental filling, kill a vampire, play poker, put up a tent

▶ What is a 'trick of the trade'? Do you know any tricks of the trade? If so, tell the rest of the class, e.g. *The best way to get your windows really clean is to dry them with newspaper.*

**Dos and don'ts**

Work in pairs. Imagine you are showing a new person around your place of work. Prepare a list of dos and don'ts. Explain all about the rules and regulations, the boss, where things go, health and safety, etc.

Read out your lists. Decide as a class where you would most/least like to work.

(As a whole class.) Tell me some of the dos and don'ts of this school.

**Driving instructor**

In pairs, role-play a learner's first driving lesson.

Student A, you are the instructor. Describe exactly what to do.
Student B, you are the learner. Follow the instructions exactly.

Here is some vocabulary to help you. (Elicit these words with mimes.)

> ignition, brake, accelerator, clutch, gear stick, steering wheel, indicator, handbrake, speedometer, seat belt, mirror, to pull out, to change gear, to accelerate, to do an emergency stop, to turn right/left, to go straight on

Find a partner who had the same role. Discuss how well the lesson went. Were the instructions easy to follow? How well did your student follow your instructions?

**Getting around**

In small groups, discuss the differences in how people do some everyday things in your country and the UK/USA/Australia/… . Here are some ideas.

> travelling on public transport, driving and the highway code, buying things, using domestic appliances, using a public telephone, eating and drinking

**Inventors**

In small groups, invent something that would be useful to you, e.g. a machine that will scratch the bit of your back you can't reach, a make-up applying robot, a machine that recycles bath water.

Draw a picture and prepare a presentation about it, describing what it is for, and giving instructions on how to use it.

### Mission

Imagine you are James Bond and you are on a mission to save the planet from a master criminal who plans to dominate the whole world. You have got a briefcase containing a recording of your instructions about the mission, including the location, name and description of the criminal. It also contains instructions on how to use the high-tech and extremely dangerous gadgets in the briefcase.

In groups, write the recorded message for James Bond. Choose five of your possessions to include as 'gadgets', e.g. a pen that fires poisonous darts when you twist the nib anti-clockwise. Swap instructions and gadgets with another group. You have one minute to memorise the instructions and learn how to use the gadgets.

Explain your mission and your gadgets to the class. The group who wrote the instructions will listen for any mistakes.

In your groups, tell each other about a film you have seen in which there were some interesting gadgets. Describe how they worked.

### House-sitting

Imagine you live in a house where everything has its idiosyncrasies, e.g. when you switch on the kettle you have to first turn off the kitchen light otherwise the dishwasher starts. In groups of three, write a list of instructions for someone coming to housesit for you while you are on holiday.

Read out your instructions. Which group seems to live in the strangest house?

In the same groups, tell each other about anything at your house which acts in an odd way, or which you think a stranger would need help with operating.

(Variation: In pairs, role-play a telephone conversation between the house-sitter and the houseowner. The house-sitter has lost the instructions. Things are getting out of control and he/she rings up the owner to check on how to do things.)

### Project

Bring a gadget to the next lesson. Work in pairs. Explain to your partner how it works. Here are some possible items.

> camera, minidisk player, game boy, mobile phone, personal organiser, camcorder

## Job search

### Work places

Work in pairs. Imagine you have a job in one of these places. Your partner will ask you yes/no questions to discover your job, e.g. A – *I work in a hospital.* B – *Do you operate on people?* A – *No. I'm not a surgeon.* B – *Do you clean the floors?* A – *No. I'm not a cleaner.*

> a hospital, Disneyland, an airport, an office, a hotel, an EFL school

### What's my job?

Work in two teams. Listen to my sentences and shout out the job. The first team to say the job each time wins a point. (Here are four ideas to start with.)

> Take two of these three times a day. (doctor) The brakes needs replacing. (mechanic)
> Are you ready to order? (waiter) Now over to Jo in the weather centre. (newsreader)

## Skills and strengths

Look at these jobs. Shout out some of the skills they need, e.g. T – *Chefs*. S – *Chefs needs to be good at organising their time.*

> actors, nurses, waiters, farmers, pilots, miners, lawyers, soldiers, artists, singers, doctors, cleaners, carpenters, journalists, bricklayers, receptionists, police officers, undertakers

Choose one of the jobs on the board. Listen to the following adjectives. Write down the ones that apply to people who are good at the job you've chosen.

> decisive, confident, motivated, creative, organised, strong, honest, flexible, hard-working, responsible, capable, inspirational, patient

What other skills does the job you've chosen need?

## Personal profiles

What is a personal profile? (Answer: a description of yourself as a professional.) Listen to this personal profile and tell me what kind of work the person does. (Possible answer: a researcher for an international company.)

> I am a *hardworking*, *energetic* and *reliable* person with a *creative* approach to tasks. I can *adapt* easily to all kinds of working environments as I am very *flexible*. An *advanced* PC user, I am also *eager* to broaden my *knowledge* and learn new *skills*. I am *articulate* and I *interact* well with colleagues. Able to work *efficiently* under pressure, I can *prioritise* my workload to meet tight *deadlines*. I am *fluent* in Russian and have an *excellent* command of German. Given the *opportunity* I will prove myself a *valuable* member of any *team*.

Listen to it again and write down the key words (in italics). Compare your list with a partner's and choose words which apply to you. Can you think of any others?

Here are some expressions from personal profiles. I'll read through them twice. Listen and write down the ones that apply to you.

> I am an excellent communicator.
> I get on well with people at all levels.
> I work well on my own or as part of a team.
> I enjoy challenges.
> I have strong leadership skills.
> I am a well-organised person.
> I enjoy learning new skills.
> I am committed to equal opportunities.
> I follow instructions well.

Write your own personal profile. Compare your profile with a partner.

## Situations vacant

In pairs, compose a short recruitment advertisement including information about the job, qualifications and experience required, and conditions of work. Swap advertisements with another pair and write some questions you would ask about the job, e.g. the number of people in the department, how many days' holiday you get. Swap partners with the same pair and role-play this telephone call.

Student A, ask about the job and request an application form.
Student B, answer questions about the job and take down Student A's details.

(This activity works well as a follow-up to the Project on the next page.)

**Job interview**

(If you do not already know about the students' professions or future career plans, ask them to tell you the job they do, or the one they would like to do. Choose two or three students who do, or would like to do, the same kind of work and put them together to prepare for a job interview for a specific position of your choosing. They should write a list of their relevant skills and strengths.

The rest of the class works in two or three groups to write interview questions for this position. Each applicant then spends ten minutes being interviewed by each group in turn. At the end of the interviews ask these questions.)

Interviewers: Who had the best qualifications and experience? Who was the most relaxed and friendly during the interview? Who gets the job?

Applicants: How did you each feel about your interview? What did you think about the attitude of the different interviewers? Do you think you'll get the job?

**Project**

► Look in the situations vacant section of a newspaper and find a job advertisement to bring to the next lesson. In class, have a look at everybody else's advert and agree the three or four most interesting ones. Work in groups, one advert for each group. Agree a list of the skills and strengths needed for the job and discuss what research you could do on the company and the job before applying.

Write a letter of application for the job. (Elicit the layout and conventions for this kind of letter. Decide if the letter should simply request an application form, enclose a CV, or give additional information.)

► Write your own CV in English and bring it to class. Include the following information.

> personal details, personal profile, education and qualifications,
> employment history, other skills, hobbies/interests, referees

In class, work in pairs or small groups. Look at another student's CV and make suggestions for improving it.

## Necessity

**Personal needs**

► (Choose students at random around the class.) Listen to what I say and repeat it, adding something that you need, e.g. T – *I'm tired.* S – *I'm tired and I need a rest.*

> I'm hungry. I'm stressed. I feel dizzy. I'm thirsty. I'm fed up with work. I'm lonely.
> I can't cope with the kids. I've got sunburn. I'm flat broke. I'm cold. I'm hot.
> I can't reach it. I'm unemployed. I'm late for a meeting. I've got a headache.

► In groups, tell each other some of the things you need in your personal life. Explain why you need them. Here are some ideas.

> shopping/groceries, household items, qualifications, money, love, holidays

Decide who in your group, and in the class as a whole, has the simplest needs.

► In groups, decide what the following people need. For each one, name the three most important things.

> holiday maker, body builder, new-born baby, student, teenager, mountaineer, entrepreneur

## Bare necessities

P I U+

In pairs, brainstorm a list of the twenty most important things that you need on a day-to-day basis and put them in order from most to least important. See how your list and order compares with another pair.

What is the bare minimum that a person needs to survive? List a few other things that people say they need, but that might not in fact be necessary.

## World needs

Work in small groups and write five ideas under each of these headings.

> what the world needs now
> what things need doing to improve this town/country
> what people need in order to live in harmony

Discuss how the needs of different countries compare.

## Jobs

► In groups, brainstorm a list of professions and corresponding abilities. Try to come up with some unusual jobs, e.g. *Explorers need to be able to ride camels. Climbers need a good head for heights.*

► In pairs, tell each other about the things you need to do/have/be for your present job, or a job that you had in the past, or one you want in the future.

## Invention

What does the saying 'Necessity is the mother of invention' mean?

In small groups, brainstorm a list of ten important inventions. Pass your list to another group. Look at the list your group receives and next to each invention write a sentence explaining why it was needed, e.g. The wheel – *It was invented because people needed to transport heavy loads.*

## Historical needs

In small groups, discuss what people needed and didn't need to do at these times, e.g. *People who lived 500 years ago needed to dry a lot of their food for the winter.*

> 50 years ago, 500 years ago, 5,000 years ago

Compare how things are different these days and make a few notes of your ideas, e.g. *Nowadays we don't need to dry things like fish because we can keep them refrigerated.*

## Jobs around the house

Work in groups of three. Student A, name a household chore. Student B, say what you need in order to do it. Student C, name the next chore, e.g.

A – *We have to clean the floor.*
B – *We need a mop and some detergent.*
C – *We have to put up a shelf.*

(Variation: For higher levels, Student A uses the structure *needs + -ing*. Student B repeats with *If ...*, e.g.

A – *The floor needs cleaning.*
B – *If the floor needs cleaning, we'll need a mop and some detergent.*
C – *A shelf needs putting up.*)

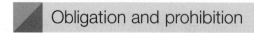

## Obligation and prohibition

E P I U+ **House rules**

In pairs, imagine that you are going to take a tenant to share your house. Agree the rules, taking into account these aspects.

> music, TV, food, the garden, visitors, pets, rent, bathroom, smoking, bills, cleaning

Explain your rules to the class, and persuade them why your rules will ensure the relationship works well. (Choose three or four pairs to present their rules to the class.)

E P I U+ **Guess the place**

Work in groups. Imagine you are in a particular place. Say one of the rules that apply, and the other students will try to guess where you are. If they can't guess, give another rule, e.g.

A – *You mustn't talk loudly.*
B – *Are you in a hospital?*
A – *No. You have to return the things you borrow.*
C – *Are you in a library?*
A – *Yes.*

E P I U+ **School rules**

In small groups, write some rules for the class and the school under these three headings.

> We have to ...   We mustn't ...   We don't have to ...

E P I U+ **Health and safety**

In groups, write a list of rules for one of these situations. (Allocate one to each group.) Choose a secretary to keep a note of your ideas under four headings: *must, mustn't, should* and *don't have to.*

> managing a restaurant, kitchen, conducting a fireworks display, looking after a baby, going trekking in the mountains

Swap lists with another group to see if they've missed anything important.

E P I U+ **Past obligation**

▶ Imagine you arrive late for an important appointment. In pairs, think of some excuses based on other obligations, e.g. *I'm sorry I'm late. The car broke down and I had to take it to the garage.* (Elicit some of the excuses to find the most creative.)

▶ In small groups, ask and answer questions about the rules at school and at home when you were a child. Here are some questions to help you.

> Did you have to ...?   Could you ...?   Were you allowed to ...?

Think about these subjects.

> smoking, punctuality, politeness, eating, studying, sport, uniform, phone, going out, homework, boyfriends and girlfriends

(This activity also works well with jobs.)

## Excuses, excuses

Fill the gaps in these sentences. (Write the text on the board gapping the words in brackets.)

> I (should) have gone to the dentist's this morning, but I overslept.
> I was (supposed) to call my sister last week, but I was too busy.

Make a list of five important things you have failed to do recently, e.g. *Check your visa. Clean your flat*. Work in pairs. Read your partner's list and find out his/her excuse for each, e.g. A – *You should have checked your visa.* B – *I know but I couldn't find my passport.* A – *You were supposed to clean your flat.* B – *Yes, but I had too much homework.*

Who had the worst excuse?

## Offers and requests

### Situations

► Listen to these ten short extracts. For each, write down three things: a) if it's an offer or a request, b) where it's happening, and c) who is speaking to whom. I'll read each sentence twice, e.g. *Would you mind turning the music down? We're trying to get to sleep. –*
*a) Request. b) Front door. c) Neighbours.*

> 1  I'll have a pound of lychees, please.
> 2  I bought this here yesterday and the strap's already broken. Can you change it?
> 3  Would you like some help with your pram, sir?
> 4  Would the owner of a fiat 500, registration number XYJ 703B, please remove it from the hotel forecourt?
> 5  Janet. Shall I give you a hand pruning this wisteria? It's growing all over the place.
> 6  Come in. Sit down. What'll you have, a glass of wine? A beer?
> 7  Oh, Francis. Will you e-mail this template to Mandy in European Research?
> 8  You wouldn't have change for the ticket machine, would you?
> 9  Would you like a free croissant with that?
> 10  Shall I make you some hot chocolate? It'll help you get to sleep.

Compare your notes with a partner. Try to write the offers and requests from memory. When you've finished, I'll read them out again so you can check your answers.

► Think of the last request and offer you made. Write them down using *him / her* instead of the person's name, e.g. *I asked him to help me fix my bike. I offered (to make) her a cup of tea.*

Work in pairs. Take turns to read your sentences. After each one, your partner will ask you a question with *who*, e.g. *Who did you ask to help you fix your bike?*

### Do you mind if ...?

Use the following prompts to make requests, e.g. *I'm cold. – Can I wear your coat? / Could I wear your coat? / Do you mind if I wear your coat?*

> I'm hungry. I'm fed up. I'm lonely. I'm stressed. I'm tired. I'm broke. It's hot in here.
> I'm thirsty. I can't reach. I can't get to sleep. I've got a headache. I need to sit down.
> There's no sugar in my tea. I don't understand. My car's broken down. I feel sick.

In pairs, use the same ideas to make offers, e.g. A – *I'm cold.* B – *I'll close the window. / Shall I close the window? / Do you want me to close the window?*

**Booking a room**

Work in pairs. Student A, you are a guest checking into a hotel. Student B, you are the receptionist. Role-play a conversation using these words. When you have finished, write the conversation down. Compare your conversation with another pair.

> single/double, en suite, 1 night/2 nights, suitcases, alarm call/time, champagne, sauna/pool, Internet

**Do me a favour**

Someone has agreed to look after your home while you're on holiday for ten days. In pairs, write a note asking them to deal with these things.

> cat, plants, TV, messages, hole in the roof, ants, neighbours, rubbish, bills

Swap your note with another pair. Now imagine you are the house-sitter. Write a note to the owner telling him/her about each of the things you had to take care of. Here's the beginning.

> Dear ____
> This has been the worst week of my life ...

**Register**

► Copy the table. Work in groups and write examples to go in the four sections of the table, using these expressions.

> Can I ...? Could I ...? Can you ...? Could you ...? Would you mind + -ing ...?
> Shall I ...? I'll ...? Give me ...? Would you like ...? Do you want ...?
> Have you got ...? Will you ...? Do you mind if I ...? Give me ...

|  | Request | Offer |
|---|---|---|
| Formal |  |  |
| Informal |  |  |

► In pairs, put the following requests in order from the most formal to the most informal. For each one, suggest
a possible relationship, e.g. *Teacher talking to a class.*

> Quiet, please.
> I'm terribly sorry to bother you, but would you mind being a little less noisy?
> Could you please be quiet?
> Shut up!
> Will you be quiet, please?
> Would you mind being a bit quieter?
> Shhhh!

► In pairs, make these expressions more formal.

> Hi. How're things? D'you want a hand? Get lost! Give us a fiver. Sugar? Come on, then.
> Leave off! I'll hold it while you tie it. Can I have one? Come here a second. What?

### Dictation

▶ Divide your page into three columns with these headings: 1) They know each other.
2) They don't know each other. 3) Either. Listen to these requests and orders. I'll read them
three times. The first time, decide which column it goes in. The second time, write it down.
The third time, check what you have written.

> Oi, you! Leave my car alone!
> I'm sorry to bother you darling, but do you think you could do the dishes?
> This soup is terrible. Can I speak to the manager?
> I don't suppose I could borrow your car for a couple of days, could I?
> Could I have change for €10?
> Can you change a tenner?
> Put your toys away at once.
> Look. If you don't stop playing your music so loud, I'll call the police!
> Why don't you leave me alone?
> Make me a sandwich, will you?

In pairs, compare your sentences and discuss what you think the relationship is between
the person speaking and the person listening. Add two more under each heading.

▶ Divide your page into two with these headings: 1) Informal and 2) Formal. Listen
to the following dialogue and write it in the first column. (Choose a student to read this
with you.)

> A: Hey, you!
> B: What, me?
> A: Yeah. Chuck us that spanner.
> B: Sure. Catch!

Work in pairs. In the second column rewrite the dialogue using more formal language, e.g.
*Hey you. – Excuse me.*

Here's another dialogue to rewrite.

> A: Do you want a hand?
> B: Oh yeah, cheers. Will you peel this?
> A: No probs. Chop it as well?
> B: No, sliced.

In your pairs, write another informal dialogue in the first column. Swap it with another
pair and write a formal translation of their dialogue.

 Permission

### May I ...?

Work in pairs. Student A, you are in Student B's house. Ask for permission using *May I ...?*
or *Can I ...?* Student B, you don't want anything touched. Refuse Student A as politely as
possible and explain why, e.g. A – *Can I open a window?* B – *I'd rather you didn't, it's very
noisy outside.*

Here are some things to talk about.

> piano, sofa, phone, TV, cake, garden, photo album, toilet, CD collection

**What's allowed?**

In small groups, discuss rights and obligations in different countries, e.g. *Are you allowed to carry a gun? At what age can you …* . Here are some ideas to help you.

> carry guns, gamble, get married, drink alcohol, hunt, drive, vote, smoke

 Telephoning

**Mobiles**

In small groups, discuss the advantages and disadvantages of mobile phones. (Elicit some ideas and write them in two columns on the board.)

In the same groups, discuss your mobile phone deal and find out whose is the best value. (If only one or two students have got a mobile phone, do this activity in open class.)

**Telephone messages**

Work in groups. I'll give each of you a situation to leave a message about on an answering machine. Write the message making up any necessary details. Then take turns to say the situation and read out your message. The rest of you, note down the details of the message such as the name and phone number of the caller, dates and times, why he/she has called etc.

> ringing about a job in the paper                reserving a seat at the theatre
> inviting a friend to a house party             arranging a babysitter
> ordering flowers for Mother's Day        calling the plumber

**Answering machines**

In small groups, compose an answering machine message for one of the following places. Include information about services and opening hours, plus options for further assistance.

> doctor's surgery, arts centre, leisure centre, airline company,
> mixed nationality company, department store, train station

**Text messages**

In pairs, translate these text messages into full English sentences.

> Y don't U call?      Want 2 speak 2 U      RU OK?      CU @ 8.30      w8'n 4 U
> gr8!                     luv U                      B :-)         I'll B L8        I'm :-(

Using a similar code, write a whole conversation between two people arranging to meet. Swap messages with another pair to write out in full.

**Projects** (www)

► Visit a mobile phone website and look for the best deal for you. Bring the information you get to class and work in small groups to discuss the deals.

► Visit the website of a large arts centre and find out what's on, including ticket prices and times of shows. Then decide what kind of show you want to see: music, theatre, exhibition, free event. In the next lesson, try to convince the other students to go with you.

# Grammar

## Adverbs

E P I U+

### Transformations

In pairs, listen to these sentences and write them down. For each one, write another sentence replacing the adjective + noun with a verb + adverb, e.g. Delia's a terrible cook – *Delia cooks terribly.*

| | |
|---|---|
| Henry's a dangerous driver. | Rebecca's a quick worker. |
| Tim's a heavy smoker. | Debby's a bad cook. |
| Kathy's a beautiful dancer. | Corinne's a slow reader. |
| Talitha's a noisy eater. | Jessica's a quiet speaker. |
| Ken's an excellent writer. | Lucy's a nice singer. |

In groups, talk about how *you* sing, drive, dance, cook, etc.

P I U+

### Silly mimes

Watch me and guess what I am miming. Write the actions down, e.g. *making a sandwich.*

drinking tea, making a pizza, driving a car, using a computer, doing the dishes, washing my hair, eating a hamburger, waiting for a bus, putting on make-up

In pairs, take turns to mime one of the actions for your partner in the manner of one of these adverbs. Try to guess the adverb your partner is miming, e.g. *You're using a computer nervously.*

sadly, gently, shyly, madly, heroically, impatiently, nervously, confidently, quietly, happily, angrily, slowly, quickly, seriously, lovingly, carefully, clumsily

P I U+

### Gradable and ungradable

In pairs, match an adjective from the first list with one from the second. What is the difference between the two lists? (Write the words from each box in two columns on the board. Re-order the adjectives in the second box when you write them up; they appear here in the correct order.)

| | |
|---|---|
| good, clever, small, hot, happy, cold, ugly, tired, difficult, hungry, funny, interesting, large | excellent, brilliant, tiny, boiling, thrilled, freezing, hideous, exhausted, impossible, famished, hilarious, fascinating, gigantic |

Compare your answers with another pair.

Look at this dialogue. (Model the emphatic stress and ask the students to repeat it.)

A – This bedroom is rather small, isn't it?
B – Small? It's absolutely tiny!

In pairs, write similar short dialogues with the words from the matching activity. (Invite pairs to read out some of their dialogues.)

**Throw and catch**

Stand in a circle. Throw this ball (a ball of paper will do) from one person to another in the circle. As you throw it, shout out an adverb. When you catch it, you've got five seconds to use the adverb in a sentence. The class decides if your sentence is correct. If it isn't, you are out of the game. The last student left standing is the winner, e.g. A (throwing) – *Fluently!* B (after catching) – *He speaks fluently.* B (throwing) – *Greedily!* C (after catching) – *He ate his dinner greedily,* etc.

**Frequency**

► Suggest some other expressions for this line. (Write *Always* and the percentages on the line and elicit the others.)

| | |
|---|---|
| Always | 100% |
| Almost always | |
| Very often | |
| Often | |
| Sometimes | |
| Rarely/Seldom | |
| Very rarely | |
| Almost never | |
| Never | 0% |

In small groups tell each other how often you do the following things, e.g. *I always walk to school. I often walk to school when the weather's nice. I very rarely walk to school.*

| | |
|---|---|
| phone my family at the weekend | iron my shirts |
| do my homework | vote at elections |
| read the Sunday papers | take a summer holiday |
| drink tea for breakfast | take public transport |

► In pairs, think of three questions to ask each other about these things, beginning *How often do you ...?*, e.g. A – *How often do you eat spaghetti?* B – *About twice a month.* Make a note of who does each thing the most and report back to the class at the end. (Read these out, allowing the students time to discuss each one.)

clean your shoes, eat spicy food, go swimming, drink coke, fly, write a letter, argue, do the dishes, go to a concert/play, laugh, get a haircut, sing

► Answer these questions using *every*, e.g. *How often does a total eclipse happen? (Once) every two years.*

| How often ... | does the world turn round? |
|---|---|
| | does the moon go round the earth? |
| | does the tide come in? |
| | do leap years occur? |
| | is the Earth hit by a comet? |
| | is there an ice age? |
| | does El Nino happen? |

## Apostrophe *s*

P | I | U+

### Dictation

I'm going to dictate a note for you to write down. I'll read the text twice.

> Hi, how's it going? Look there's a party at Steve's place. He's invited some musicians round. Tom's going, and his flatmate, what's her name, Tracey. She's a guitarist and she's got a great voice. It's been ages since I went to Steve's. It's going to be lots of fun. He's cooking a curry and he's got some beers in, but let's take a bottle, too. There's an off licence that's just opened near Tom's. It's called Joe's Wines. Let's meet there at seven. OK, see you later.

Compare your text with a partner. How many times did you write *'s*? There should be twenty. Decide whether each *'s* is a) an abbreviation of *is*, b) an abbreviation of *has*, c) an abbreviation of *us*, or d) a possessive *'s*.

P | I | U+

### Possessive *'s*

In pairs, discuss what you know about each other, e.g. *Carmita's hair is curly. Henri's job is interesting.*

Write a list of five guesses about the other students in the class, e.g. *Carmita's favourite activity is watching TV.* Read out your guesses and see if they are true.

P | I | U+

### Celebrity *'s*

Here are some words for describing people. In small groups, write pairs of sentences about famous people using the possessive *'s* and contractions of *be/have*, e.g. *Leonardo di Caprio's eyes are blue – Leonardo di Caprio's got blue eyes.* (You may like to add a few features to this list for describing celebrities that are well known to your students.)

> blue eyes, red hair, big teeth, long legs, curly hair,
> green eyes, big muscles, nice voice, bushy eyebrows

## Articles

P | I | U+

### A, an and the

► (Write up the first sentence in this sequence and elicit the others by asking questions with *where*, e.g. *Where's the page?*)

> There's a word on a page. The page is in a book. The book is on a table. The table is in a room. The room is in a house. The house is in a street. The street is in a city ...

In small groups, take turns to add to these sequences in a similar way.

> There's a worm in an apple ...          There's a bee on a flower ...
> There's a flea on a dog ...             There's a fish in a pond ...

► In pairs, write a sentence containing *a/an* and *the*, e.g. *I had an appointment with the doctor. The car had a flat tyre.* On a separate piece of paper, write the sentence out again with gaps for every word except *a/an* and *the*. Pass your gapped sentence to another pair. Fill in the gaps in the sentence you receive in any way you can, e.g. *There is an apple on the table. The woman wore a blue hat.*

**There was an old lady**

I'm going to tell you a nursery rhyme about an old lady who swallowed some animals. It begins *There was an old lady who swallowed a fly.* Why do you think she swallowed the fly? (Write the next two lines at the bottom of the board.)

> I don't know why she swallowed the fly.
> Perhaps she'll die.

What did she do next? (Elicit ideas, and then give the next line of the rhyme: *There was an old lady who swallowed a spider.*)

Why did she swallow the spider? (Elicit ideas and then add this line above the two others at the bottom of the board.)

> She swallowed the spider to catch the fly.
> I don't know why she swallowed the fly.
> Perhaps she'll die.

What did she do next? (Elicit ideas, and then give the next line of the rhyme: *There was an old lady who swallowed a bird.*)

Why did she swallow the bird? (Elicit ideas, and then continue to add the lines of the rhyme above the others, continuing with the same sequence until the rhyme is finished, i.e. *She swallowed the bird to catch the spider.* The rest of the sequence is: cat, dog, goat, cow, horse. At the end, ask the students to recite the rhyme to each other in pairs. Anyone who is confident can recite the whole thing for the class from memory.)

**Geography quiz**

Work in four or five teams. Each team must choose a different continent, not including Australia or Antarctica. I'm going to name some different geographical features. Make a note of one example belonging to the continent you chose, e.g. *A mountain range – The Blue Mountains* (Australia).

> river, desert, lake, island group, capital city, mountain range, mountain, sea, forest/jungle, man-made feature

Score a point for every correct example you name. If a team cannot name an example, the other teams can get an extra point by naming one in that continent.

## Be/Get used to

**Prompts**

In pairs, listen to these prompts and agree an explanation using *be (not) used to*. Write it down, e.g. *I'm so tired. – I'm not used to working shifts. / I can't get used to working shifts. / I don't think I'll ever get used to working shifts.*

| | |
|---|---|
| Don't touch my dog! | It was so embarrassing. |
| Slow down! | Elephants don't like zoos. |
| I'm afraid I've crashed your car. | Dominique is drunk already. |
| I find him difficult to live with. | I can't drink this tea. |
| They don't like London. | This country is too cold for me. |

Compare your explanations with another pair. Which do you like better?

P  I  U+ **Write home**

In pairs, write a letter from a young student who has gone abroad to study and is writing to his/her parents telling them about life in a new city. Use different forms of *be/get used to*, e.g. *I've got used to drinking tea with milk, but I can't get used to the coffee. I'm getting used to driving on the left. I'll never get used to the weather.*

Write about these aspects of life.

> manners, fashion, shopping, food, pets, traffic, language, household appliances, the weather

## Comparatives and superlatives

P  I  U+ **Preferences**

► In pairs, discuss these questions. (Read them out one at a time and allow a few minutes for discussion.)

> Which do you prefer, tea or coffee?
> Who do you think is more handsome/beautiful, (choose two celebrities)?
> Which do you prefer, spring or autumn? Why?
> Do you prefer to express yourself by speaking or by writing?
> Do you prefer cats or dogs? Why?
> Do you prefer sunrise or sunset? Why?
> Would you rather be rich and ugly, or poor and good looking? Why?

► In pairs, write two questions about preferences. Choose one each, and survey the rest of the class. (Invite students to report their results.)

P  I  U+ **Countries**

► In groups of three or four, discuss these questions about the UK/USA.

> Is the UK/USA hotter or colder than your country? How much?
> Is it wetter/greyer, etc?
> Is it cheaper / more expensive?
> What are the differences between your country and the UK/USA?
> Which things are better in your country than in the UK/USA?

► In pairs, compare two countries you know well using these ideas.

> big, small, developed, mixed, green, corrupt, hot, cold,
> mountainous, expensive, tolerant, football crazy, safe, rich

(Variation: Give a country to each pair of students. Ask them to write a list of comparisons between that country and the country they are in now. They read out their comparisons and the others try to guess the country.)

P  I  U+ **Yes, but ...**

In two teams, write ten short sentences containing an adjective, e.g. *Liverpool is a good football team.* Take turns to read out one of your sentences. Someone in the other team has to respond immediately with a comparative, beginning 'Yes, but ...', e.g. *Yes, but Barcelona is better.*

**Circle comparatives**

Shout out words to go in this group. (Choose one of the following categories and write the elicited words on the board in a circle.)

animals, countries, sports, methods of transport

In small groups, you have five minutes to write as many comparisons as you can, e.g. *Dogs are more intelligent than cats.*

Read out your sentences. Each group gets one point for every grammatically correct comparison that no other group has written. You can challenge another group's comparison if it's factually wrong or if it contains a grammatical mistake.

(Variation: Give a different category to each group.)

**Appearances** ⚠

In pairs, compare your appearances and your possessions, e.g. *I've got smaller hands. You've got more organised notes.* Here are some ideas.

longer nails, more pockets, a more interesting uncle, a heavier bag, neater writing, bigger feet, smaller hands, shorter hair, darker eyes, bushier eyebrows, more colourful clothes, newer shoes

**Advertising agency**

Tell me things which are often advertised on TV. (Write the elicited list on the board.)

In small groups, choose one of these things and think of a new brand. Write a radio advert explaining why it's better than its competitors, e.g. *For the whitest teeth buy Afterglo. It whitens your teeth and leaves your breath fresher than mountain air. It's more effective than all its leading competitors. Choose Afterglo, for the brightest, most confident smile.*

Read out your advert to the class. When you're listening to the other groups' adverts, make some notes for a complaint to the Advertising Standards Agency, e.g. *The advert says it's more effective than other toothpastes, but it contains much more sugar than other brands to make it taste better.*

**The sooner the better**

Work in pairs. I'm going to read the beginnings of ten sentences. Quickly agree an ending and write it down. You won't have much time before I say the next one. If you haven't finished, leave it and start the next, e.g. T – *The earlier we leave* ... S – *the sooner we'll arrive.*

| | |
|---|---|
| The more you study ... | The cheaper the hotel ... |
| The more he drinks ... | The hotter it gets ... |
| The less you know ... | The older he gets ... |
| The more we give him ... | The less she eats ... |
| The longer we waited ... | The more interesting the work ... |

Compare your endings with another pair. How many are similar?

In pairs, write two more beginnings and pass them on to another pair to complete.

**The same as or different?** ⚠

Compare your possessions and abilities with the students sitting on either side of you using *the same as* or *different from*, e.g. *My trainers are the same make as Luteka's. My first language is different from Abida's.*

## As ... as

Take turns to ask me questions about the prices of these things in the UK/USA/Australia/... .
After each answer, write a sentence comparing the price with the price in your country, e.g.
*Cigarettes are almost twice as expensive in the Australia.*

> food, alcohol, clothes, cigarettes, transport, entertainment, accommodation, cars

Here are some expressions to help you.

| | |
|---|---|
| not quite<br>half<br>twice<br>three times<br>not nearly | as expensive as |

Compare your sentences with a partner.

In pairs, write some more comparisons, e.g. *It's not nearly as sunny in England as it is in my country. There are (more than) twice as many people in my country.*

## Opinions

► Work in groups. I'm going to give each group a question to discuss. Choose one person
to make notes and another who will use the notes to report back to the class.

> What are the biggest problems facing mankind at the moment?
> Why is the USA the most powerful country in the world?
> What are the most difficult things about learning English?
> What are the best and worst things about living in this country?

► In pairs, tell your partner about your opinions and experiences of these things.

| | |
|---|---|
| The most amazing thing ... | The most exciting film ... |
| The best book ... | The nicest person in the world ... |
| The strangest experience ... | The smallest thing I own ... |
| The most important person ... | The hottest/coldest I've ever been was ... |

## Class survey

I'm going to dictate one question to each student. Mingle and ask all the other students
your question. Make a note of their answers.

| | |
|---|---|
| Who has been in this school the longest? | Who has visited the most countries? |
| Who drinks the most coffee? | Who has the shortest surname? |
| Who has the nearest birthday to today? | Who speaks the most languages? |
| Who has got the longest eyelashes? | Who sleeps the least? |
| Who comes from the biggest family? | Who has the most CDs? |
| Who is wearing the most expensive shoes? | Who has eaten the most unusual thing? |

## Favourites

In pairs, use comparatives and superlatives to tell each other about your favourite things,
e.g. *I like crime novels because they usually have the most exciting stories.* Here are some ideas.

> book, song, film, sport, vegetable, actor, animal, café, colour, pizza, person, drink

**Round Britain quiz**

I'm going to give you the answers to a superlative quiz about the UK. Write them down in a column on the left hand side of a piece of paper. Then work in pairs. Can you guess the questions? Write them next to the answers.

> 1  What is the highest mountain? (Ben Nevis, 1,343 m)
> 2  Who is the richest person? (The Duke of Westminster, €8.2 billion)
> 3  What is the furthest country from the UK? (New Zealand)
> 4  What is the second biggest city? (Birmingham, 2.3 million)
> 5  Where is the largest lake? (Scotland, Loch Lomond, 312 km²)
> 6  What is the longest river? (The Severn, 322 km)
> 7  Where are the heaviest smokers? (Manchester)
> 8  What is the most common surname? (Smith)
> 9  What is the tallest office building? (Canary Wharf, 244 m)
> 10  What is the busiest airport? (Heathrow, 54.5 million passengers per year)
> 11  Which is the longest running soap opera? (Coronation Street, since 1960)
> 12  What is the most popular daily newspaper? (The Sun)

Compare your questions with another pair.

In pairs, think of five questions with superlatives about a country you know well. Give the questions to another pair to answer.

**Sporting superlatives**

These are all world records in different sports. Work in pairs and guess what the sports and records are. Ask a question for each one using superlatives, e.g. 375 – Brian Lara. *What's the highest score made by an international cricketer? (375) Who has scored the most runs in an international cricket match? (Brian Lara).*

> 5 times – Brazil (most football World Cups)
> 9 times – Martina Navratilova (most Wimbledon championships)
> 193 moves / 24 hours – Stepak v Mashian (longest chess match)
> 9.78 seconds – Tim Montgomery (fastest 100 m)
> 8.95 m – Mike Powell (longest jump)
> 22.63 m – Natalya Lisovskaya (furthest women's shot put)
> 190 kg – Edmilson da Silva Dantas (heaviest weightlift)
> 17 years – Boris Becker (youngest Wimbledon men's champion)
> 2.48 m – Suleiman Ali Nashnush (tallest basketball player)

In pairs, write two more questions about the best (and worst) in the world of sport. See if anybody in the class knows the answers.

 ## Conditionals – first

**Country game**

Take it in turns to name a country and a student. The person you name has to say what they'll do if they go to the country you name, e.g. T – *India, Alyosha.* Alyosha – *If I go to India, I'll visit Bollywood. Spain, Masha.* Masha – *If I go to Spain, I'll go walking in the Pyrenees.*

**Manifestoes**

In groups, prepare a short policy statement for your (silly) political party, e.g. *If you vote for us, we'll ban the use of mobile phones in restaurants.*

**If it's sunny ...**

▶ Work in groups of three or four. Take turns to continue one of these sequences. After each sentence, the group should ask what will happen next, e.g.

A – *If it's sunny, I'll go to the park.*
Group – *What will you do if you go to the park?*
B – *If I go to the park, I'll play cricket.*
Group – *What will you do if you win?*
C – *If we win, we'll go to the pub.*
Group – *What will you do if you go to the pub?*

| | | |
|---|---|---|
| If it rains tomorrow ... | If he rings ... | If we save enough ... |
| If I study hard ... | If we win the match ... | If I learn Polish ... |

(Write these phrases on the board in two columns. Re-order the phrases in the second box.)
In pairs, think of connections between these two groups of expressions, and write sentences, e.g. *If we move house, we'll get one with a garden.*

| |
|---|
| move house, holiday, good job, not drink, be positive, bicycle, cat, eat less, miss flight, Portuguese, go out, baby |

| |
|---|
| garden, suntan, save money, be thirsty, make friends, get fit, mice, lose weight, holiday, Brazil, cinema, stop work |

▶ I'm going to read the endings for some sentences. Write the whole sentence, beginning with *If ...* , e.g. *... you'll regret it.* – *If you don't listen to my advice, you'll regret it.*

| | | |
|---|---|---|
| ... you'll hurt yourself. | ... we'll be late. | ... it'll taste better. |
| ... you'll catch a cold. | ... I'll let you know. | ... there'll be trouble. |

Compare your sentences with a partner.

In pairs, write five more endings. Swap them with another pair, write the beginnings to the ones you receive and hand back the whole sentences. Did the other pair write the beginnings you were expecting?

**Functions**

▶ Here is a list of six functions. (Write them on the board.)

| |
|---|
| prediction, offer, warning, threat, advice, suggestions |

I'm going to dictate six sentences. Write them down and decide which function they have. (Read out the sentences in a different order; they appear in the same order as the functions.)

| |
|---|
| 1 If we don't leave now, we'll miss the train. |
| 2 If you want, I'll do the dishes. |
| 3 If you touch that wire, you'll get an electric shock. |
| 4 If you don't stop doing that, I'll get angry. |
| 5 If you explain why you did it, he'll understand. |
| 6 If you turn it round the other way, it'll fit. |

In pairs, compare your answers. Then write another conditional sentence for each function.

▶ In groups, think of some situations where people make bargains with each other. Write an appropriate *If ...* sentence for each. Read out your sentences for other groups to guess who is speaking to whom, e.g. *If you're good, I'll buy you an ice-cream* (parent to child).

E P I U+ **Anxiety role-plays**

Work in pairs, A and B. Student A is very adventurous; Student B is very anxious. In your pairs, role-play a discussion between two good friends about the situation I give you, e.g.

A – *I'm going to tour the Amazon.*
B – *What will you do if you catch malaria?*
A – *Don't worry. If I catch malaria, I'll go to see a local doctor.*
B – *But what if you're in the middle of the jungle?*
A – *If I'm in the jungle, I'll see an Amazonian Indian doctor.*
B – *What will happen if you get lost?*
A – *If I get lost ...*

---

1 You are going on holiday to South America, where you will spend six months taking photographs of the wildlife and landscapes, including the jungles, mountains, sea and desert.

2 You are giving up a well-paid job to become an art student in Paris.

3 You are getting married to a singer in a rock and roll band that has a reputation for very bad behaviour.

---

E P I U+ **Superstitions**

Are people in your country very superstitious? What are they superstitious about? What about you?

In pairs, write superstitions for some of these words, e.g. *If you break a mirror, you'll have seven years' bad luck.* Make them up if you don't know any.

---

mirror, black cat, ladder, birthday cake candles, itchy ear, itchy hand, salt, sneezing, spider, the number thirteen, the weather

---

Join with another pair to make small groups. Compare your superstitions. What other superstitions can you think of?

 Conditionals – second

E P I U+ **What if ...**

▶ Supposing you could meet anyone you wanted, alive or dead, who would it be? Why? What would you say to him/her?

If you could live in another place and time in history, what would it be?

▶ In small groups, brainstorm some endings for these sentences. Choose the best from your group and write the whole sentence down. (Ask the groups to read out their ideas and invite the class to choose their favourites.)

---

If the world was flat ...
If we were all clones ...
If you had two heads ...
If time travel was possible ...
If nobody knew how to read ...

If animals could speak ...
If cows could fly ...
If money grew on trees ...
If there was no money ...
If everyone was telepathic ...

---

▶ If I gave you one million euros, what would you do with it? Write a list of five things. Read out your list. Who does the class think should get the money?

**If ...**

► Work in pairs. Listen to these situations and write what would happen if the situation was different, e.g. It's raining; we'll have to cancel the barbecue. – *If it wasn't raining, we'd have a barbecue. If it was sunny, we'd have a barbecue.*

> I don't know the answer so I can't tell you.
> He gets headaches because he works so hard.
> We don't have enough space for a piano.
> She's ill. She can't come to the party.
> Life's easy because we both have well-paid jobs.
> He's not tall enough to be a policeman.
> I can't give you a lift because I haven't got a car.
> She's so rude it's not surprising they don't like her.

► In pairs, tell your partner about things in your life you would change if you had the opportunity, e.g. *If I had more money, I'd buy a car and do more travelling. If I didn't have to work in the evenings, I'd do more exercise and get fit.*

## World affairs ⚠

In small groups, brainstorm some current world news stories and suggest improvements using the second conditional, e.g. *If we all voted him out of office, the country would be a safer place.*

## Advice

In pairs, give each other advice for these problems, beginning *If I were you, I'd ...*

> I want to give up smoking. | I'm fed up doing temporary jobs.
> I love her, but she never calls. | My dog keeps biting people.
> I can't get to sleep at night. | Our house is cold and damp.
> I keep dropping things. | English spelling is so hard!
> My flatmate's really untidy. | My hair won't stay flat.

## I wish and If only

In pairs, rewrite these sentences with *I wish / If only* in two ways, one with a past tense and the other with *would*, e.g. It's raining. – 1) *I wish / If only it wasn't raining.* 2) *I wish / If only it would stop raining.*

> She's singing that awful song again. | I've had a nasty cold all week.
> You're unemployed. | He's late for the meeting again.
> It's cold outside. | They never write to us.
> The lift is still not working. | The streets here are filthy.

## A better place to live

In pairs, write five sentences beginning *I wish ...* about the town or city where you live in order to make it a better place to live, e.g. *I wish the buses ran all through the night so I didn't have to take a taxi home.*

Join with another pair. Discuss your sentences and decide which are the best five of your ideas from your combined lists. Then join with another group of four students and choose the best five ideas again. Choose someone from your group to write your ideas up on the board. As a class, decide on the best five sentences.

(Variation: This activity also works well with ideas for improving the school.)

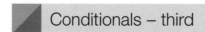

## Conditionals – third

E P I U· **The unreal past**

In pairs, look at the following sentences and decide whether the people in each situation feel happy about what happened, unhappy about it, or just neutral, e.g.

Ray went to the party.
– *If Ray hadn't gone to the party, he wouldn't have met Maggie* (happy, because he met her).
– *If he hadn't gone to the party, he would have felt better the next morning* (unhappy, because he went to the party and now he is tired / has a hangover).
– *If Ray hadn't gone to the party, he'd have gone clubbing instead* (neutral, because he'd have spent the night dancing anyway).

| | |
|---|---|
| Terry moved to New York. | He didn't know she was coming. |
| James crashed his car. | Vera lost her lottery ticket. |
| Sonya went to Japan. | Irene didn't have a spare key. |
| Roger didn't pass the exam. | Tracy couldn't sell her house. |

Imagine you were the person in some of the situations. Work with a partner and write some sentences to express regret. Use *If only / I wish* and *should (not) have done*, e.g. *If only / wish I hadn't gone to the party. I shouldn't have drunk so much.*

E P I U· **Mountain rescue**

(Write up the sentences below in random order on the board.) These situations are all connected to the same adventure. Work in groups and put them in order. Imagine you were stuck on the mountain. Write two sentences for each situation, one using *If only / I wish ...* and one using *should (not) have done*, e.g. *I wish / If only we hadn't got lost. We should have stayed at home. We shouldn't have been so careless.*

| |
|---|
| We didn't tell anyone at the hostel where we were going. |
| Leo forgot to pack a compass. |
| We left later than planned. |
| The cloud came down, but we decided to continue walking. |
| We lost the path. |
| Kathy fell and broke her leg. |
| No one had a mobile phone. |
| Ben tried to go back down the mountain. |
| All we had was a bar of chocolate. |
| Nobody had a torch. |

What order did your group decide on? Talk together and decide what happened next. Did everyone survive?

E P I U· **Speculation** ⚠

▶ In pairs, talk about your childhood and speculate about how things might have been different, e.g. *If I had worked harder at school, I could have got a better job. If we had lived in the country instead of a big city, my parents wouldn't have worried about my safety so much.*

▶ In pairs, think about some recent events in the news. Discuss how they might have been different, e.g. *If they had built the bridge properly, it wouldn't have fallen down in the earthquake. If the referee had been fair, Brazil would have won the football match.*

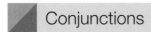

## Conjunctions

### And, but and because

In pairs, take turns to continue these sentences, using *and*, *but* and *because*, e.g.

I'm tired ...
A – *I'm tired and I'm going to bed.*
B – *I'm tired, but I've got to finish this essay.*
A – *I'm tired because I've been up all night studying.*

| | | |
|---|---|---|
| The coffee is good ... | He married Susan ... | Simon is sick ... |
| They got lost ... | I'm learning English ... | They went to India ... |
| My teacher is nice ... | Glenda bought a car ... | I went to the shop ... |

### Expanding sentences

(Write *and*, *but*, *because* and *so* on the board.) I'm going to give you a short sentence. In turn, repeat it and add one of these conjunctions and a clause. Continue around the class, expanding the sentence with each turn. If you forget the sentence, you are out of the game. (When the sentence gets too long, start a new one.)

T – *I had a dog.*
A – *I had a dog, but he died.*
B – *I had a dog, but he died, so I bought a cat.*
C – *I had a dog, but he died, so I bought a cat because I needed the company.*

### Despite, although and however

▶ Look at this example. (Write it on the board.)

Bill is poor but he's healthy.
– *Despite his poverty, Bill is healthy.*
– *Although he's poor, Bill is healthy.*
– *Bill is poor. However, he's healthy.*

In pairs, change these sentences in the same way.

| | | |
|---|---|---|
| Arnold is strong, but gentle. | It's raining, but it's not cold. | They're rich, but unhappy. |
| It's expensive, but useless. | It's cold, but we have to go. | Granny's old, but she's agile. |

Think of five similar sentences that are true for you. Tell your partner.

▶ In pairs, finish these sentences.

| | |
|---|---|
| Despite the speed we were driving ... | Despite being completely exhausted ... |
| Despite the fact that I am a single parent ... | Despite her cold ... |
| Despite his good looks ... | Despite not speaking Italian ... |
| Despite the problems we face ... | Despite having ten children ... |

### Or (else)

(Do this activity in open class. Choose students at random and ask them to add to the following sentences as you read them out, beginning with *or (else)*, e.g. You'd better not drink anymore ... *or (else) you won't be able to drive.*)

| | |
|---|---|
| Don't touch that wire. | I have to have a shower every morning. |
| You should study harder. | Listen to me. |
| Don't forget to send it today. | You'd better get some sleep. |
| Stop thinking about the exam. | I'd better pay these bills. |

**Life plans**

▶ Look at this pattern and write some more sentences that are true for you, e.g. *When it stops raining, I'll go out. As soon as he phones, I'll let you know.*

| when |  |  |
| --- | --- | --- |
| as soon as |  |  |
| until | + present ⟶ future |
| before |  |  |

Write some more examples using these verbs.

arrive, end (this lesson), start work, get up, finish job, go out, finish, be ready, get married, have dinner, do homework

▶ In pairs, tell each other about your own expectations using *going to* for plans, e.g. *As soon as my English is good enough, I'm going to go back home and get a good job.*

In pairs, continue this sequence, e.g. *As soon as I pass my exams I'll go to college. When I leave college I'm going to go travelling. I'll keep travelling until my money runs out ...* Try to make it go somewhere interesting, e.g. into an extremely adventurous life, a lucky one, etc.

pass exams ⟶ leave college ⟶ go travelling ⟶ live in India ...

## Copular verbs

**Looks**

▶ (Draw these faces on the board.) How do these people look? (Answers: happy, mischievous, unhappy, angry.)

Draw faces to demonstrate the following adjectives. (Write the adjectives on the board scattered in a circle. Students drawn them in any order they choose.) Ask your partner to say how each face looks.

tired, confused, bored, scared, excited, embarrassed

▶ In pairs, discuss how these people might look and feel?

| | |
| --- | --- |
| He's just won a marathon. | She's got a terrible hangover. |
| They're playing poker. | She's just fallen over in the street. |
| They're about to take an important exam. | They're about to get married. |
| He's bought a new sports car. | She's going to complain to the manager. |
| It hasn't eaten anything for days. | He's just seen a ghost. |

## The senses

▶ In two groups, write three or four short sentences for each of these things to describe how they look, taste, smell, feel or sound, e.g. *It tastes sweet. It feels sticky.*

> concrete, sandpaper, hair, diamond, clown, lemon, baby, brick, ice-cream, porridge, cashmere, curry, garlic, roses, raw fish, antiques, bagpipes

(Give some help by writing up some adjectives if necessary.)

> sour, cold, silly, hard, bitter, tasty, spicy, sweet, smooth, soft, fresh, nice, oily, dusty, out of tune, disgusting, hot, cute, beautiful, exciting, loud

Take turns to read out a description for the other group to guess what you are describing.

▶ Work on your own. Write a description of two things and see if the class can guess what they are.

## But in fact ...

I'm going to dictate the endings of some sentences. Write them down and add a beginning, using *look, seem, taste* or *feel*, e.g. ... but in fact he's quite young. – *He looks old, but in fact he's quite young.*

> ... but in fact it's good for you.
> ... but in fact he's a big softy really.
> ... but in fact my temperature's normal.
> ... but in fact cats love it.
> ... but in fact it tastes OK.
>
> ... but in fact it's extremely dangerous.
> ... but in fact he's quite nice.
> ... but in fact she's not really.
> ... but in fact he looks calm and relaxed.
> ... but in fact it really goes fast.

Compare your ideas with a partner.

Work together to write another two endings and pass them to the next pair. Add beginnings to the ones you receive.

## Demonstrative adjectives and pronouns

### Realia

In pairs, use the things and colours in the classroom to make sentences for your partner to guess, e.g. A – *This is red; that is green.* B – *Files.* A – *These are blue; those are black.* A – *Pens.*

### Whose is this?

(Write these question prompts on the board.) Take turns to point to another student's possessions and ask me one of these questions.

> Whose is this ...?   Whose are these ...?   Whose is that ...?   Whose are those ...?

I will say the wrong person's name. That person should correct me, and then ask the next question. (You may want to write the following example on the board.)

Pedro – *Whose is this pen?*
T – *It's Julia's.*
Julia – *No, that's not my pen. This is my pen. Whose are those shoes?*
T – *They're Ronaldo's.*
Ronaldo – *No, those aren't my shoes. These are my shoes. Whose is this file?*

### Hotter and colder

Try to find the object in the classroom that I'm thinking of. Point and ask me questions, e.g. *Is it this book? Is it that chair?* As your guesses get closer to it, I'll say 'hotter' and as they get further away, I'll say 'colder'.

Play the same game in pairs, taking turns to ask the questions.

## Future

### Prediction ⚠

▶ What methods of predicting the future do you know of? Do you think there is any truth in any of these methods? Have you ever had your future predicted? What was the prediction and did it come true?

▶ What are the signs of the zodiac? (Write them on the board. See page 147.) Form pairs or small groups according to your star signs. (Some students will have to work on their own.) Write two horoscopes: a good one for your sign and a bad one for the sign that comes after yours. Include these subjects.

> health, money, work, family, travel, love

▶ Work with a partner and read each other's palms according to these principles. Read the palm of the hand your partner doesn't write with.

> 1  Life line – If this is long and thick, you will have a long, healthy life. If it's broken, you will suffer an illness.
> 2  Head line – This shows how clever you are. The longer and thicker it is, the more intelligent you are.
> 3  Fate line – This is usually a vague line. It indicates how lucky you will be, and how healthy.
> 4  Heart line – If this is made up of a lot of lines, it means you will have lots of relationships.
> 5  Number of children – This shows how many children you can expect to have.

▶ Agree a list of ten major changes that you think will take place during the next hundred years. Include these things.

> technology, war and peace, culture, economics, Europe, ecology

▶ In pairs, tell each other about your hopes and plans for the future, including marriage, ambitions, home, travel and work. Use these expressions. (Write them on the board.)

> I think I'll ...      Maybe I'll ...      I hope I'll ...
> I'll never ...      I expect I'll ...      I'll probably ...

▶ In small groups, write five questions with *Do you think ... + will* that you might ask a friend, e.g. *Do you think you'll ever settle down somewhere?* Here are some possible topics to ask about.

> job, accommodation, children, money, English, fame

## Spontaneous decisions

► We're going to have a class party next week. What will you bring or do? (This works best if you really are having a party, but an imaginary one will do. Later in the lesson, ask the students to remind you of what they are *going to* bring or do.)

► Imagine two friends are having a conversation. I'll tell you what one of them says; suggest a helpful response, e.g. T – *My car won't start.* S – *I'll give you a lift.*

| | |
|---|---|
| Sorry, I'm too busy to chat at the moment. | That's the doorbell. |
| Ouch! I've cut myself. | Here's €50. |
| Don't forget it's Mum's birthday next week. | Quick! Someone's just collapsed. |
| I asked you to tidy the flat. | The photocopier's broken down. |
| I think the baby's crying. | I need a hand with this shelf. |

## Future continuous

In pairs, ask and answer questions about what you'll be doing at these times, e.g. A – *What will you be doing (this time) tomorrow?* B – *I'll be relaxing at home.*

> this time tomorrow, this time next week, this time next month, this time next year, in ten years' time, when I see you again

## Future perfect

► In groups of three or four, discuss the changes you expect by the end of the twenty-first century. Appoint a secretary and write a short paragraph about each one, e.g. *Scientists will have discovered a new way to travel.*

Here are some verbs to help you. (Write them on the board.)

> develop, discover, become, invent, build, learn

Compare your ideas with another group.

► What do you think you will have learnt by the end of the lesson/week/term? Discuss this with your partner, with reference to the course book and/or your copy of the syllabus.

In the same pairs, discuss what you think you will have achieved in five/ten/twenty years.

# Gerunds

## Likes and dislikes

► In pairs, find out about your partner's likes and dislikes, e.g. A – *What do you like doing in the evening?* B – *I like cooking.* A – *Do you like doing the dishes?* B – *No. I hate doing the dishes.*

Use these words to help you.

> do/evening, eat/breakfast, watch/TV, play/sport, read/book, do/weekend, talk/friends

Tell me a few of the things you found out about your partner.

► On your own, write five sentences about yourself using a gerund. Choose from among these adjectives, e.g. *Dancing makes me feel happy.*

> sad, tired, excited, sick, dizzy, proud, happy, insecure, relaxed, guilty, embarrassed, angry

**My opinion**

► Work in three teams. I'll give each team three adjectives. Use these adjectives with a gerund to write sentences, e.g. stupid – *Drink driving is stupid.*

> 1 tiring, boring, stressful
> 2 dangerous, exciting, unhealthy
> 3 illegal, healthy, relaxing

Read out your adjectives. The rest of the class will guess what gerund you have written.

► In pairs, write down four opinions using a gerund, e.g. *Working more than 40 hours a week should be illegal.*

Choose one of the opinions each and do a survey of the class to find out how many students agree.

**Speaking personally**  ⚠

► Write sentences which are true for you, using these verbs, and gerunds, e.g. *I'm going to keep trying until I pass the FCE exam.*

> keep, involve, start, stop, suggest, imagine, regret, miss, practise, consider, (not) mind

Compare your sentences with your partner. Ask about anything that surprises or interests yo◄

► Listen to these questions and write down your answers, being as honest as you can. When you have finished, compare your sentences with your partner.

> Is there any activity you feel you should give up?
> Do you ever imagine being someone else? Who?
> What childhood activity do you miss doing?
> What unusual activity do you enjoy doing?
> What are two things you can't stand other people doing?
> What have you always dreamt of doing?
> What are you looking forward to doing?

► Work in small groups and listen to these prompts. Each member of the group should repeat the prompt and finish the sentence truthfully. Make a note of the most interesting things you learn about your colleagues, e.g. *Pavel's thinking of going to China next year.*

> I'm good at ...                    I often dream about ...
> I'm keen on ...                    Sometimes I get fed up with ...
> I'm thinking of ...                I'm interested in ...
> I get very excited about ...       I sometimes regret not ...

**What's it for?**

► In pairs, discuss what these objects are used for, e.g. *A kettle is used for boiling water.*

> sieve, stamp, pin, brush, whistle, bottle, corkscrew, padlock, scissors, brick, rope, iron, ruler, torch, scarf, rubber band, camera, compass, CD

► In small groups, think of unusual uses for a normal object. Write down ten uses and pu◄ them in order with the least likely first and the most likely last. I'll ask you to read out the uses one at a time. After each use, the rest of the class will try to guess the object, e.g. (A shoe) *It can be used for storing pasta.*

## Going to

### Plans

► Make a note of what are you going to do at these times.

> after class, tonight, tomorrow, on Saturday, next week, next year

Mingle, and find someone who is going to do some of the same things as you, e.g. *Maria and I are both going ice skating on Saturday.* (Elicit some responses.)

► On your own, think of an activity that people often do at the weekend. Tell me what it is. (If someone repeats an activity that another student has already said, tell them they have to think of another one and come back to them when they've done so.) Mingle and find out how many students in the class are going to do the thing you thought of.

► Do you make New Year's resolutions? Tell us a few typical resolutions people make.

In pairs, imagine it is New Year's Eve. Write down three resolutions for somebody famous, e.g. *I'm going to tell fewer lies to the newspapers. I'm going to get a better lawyer.*

Compare your resolutions with another pair. Can they guess the famous person?

### Evidence

► Watch me and guess what I'm going to do. (Mime preparations for these activities.)

> do the dishes, play football, go to a disco, be late, watch television,
> have a cup of tea, make an omelette, work on a computer, play the piano

In small groups, think of some similar mimes for the class to guess what you're going to do.

► Work in two teams. Listen to these sentences and tell me exactly what I'm going to do. If you're right, your team gets a point.

> I've put on my coat and hat. (I'm going to go for a walk.)
> The phone is ringing. (I'm going to ignore it.)
> I've got the ingredients. (I'm going to make a cake.)
> I've bought the tickets. (I'm going to catch a train.)
> I've bought flowers. (I'm going to a funeral.)
> It's late and I'm tired. (I'm going to ask you to leave.)
> I've got the tools. (I'm going to build a shed.)
> There's a bottle of wine on the table. (I'm going to open it.)
> The kitchen's full of dirty dishes. (I'm going to buy a dishwasher.)
> I'm absolutely exhausted. (I'm going to have a cup of coffee.)
> I've got a headache. (I'm going to lie down.)
> It's raining. (I'm going to bring the laundry in.)
> There's a great film on TV tonight. (I'm going to record it.)
> I'm hungry. (I'm going to have some toast.)
> I've lost my keys. (I'm going to climb in through the window.)

### Policy statement

Imagine you are the leader of a newly elected government. You have just finished a cabinet meeting and are presenting your policies to parliament, e.g. *We are going to tax the rich.* Work together in groups and write your policies.

(Variation: Get different groups to represent different political parties and to heckle each other's presentations. This is also a good opportunity to practice *was/were going to*, e.g. *But you said you were going to cut taxes!*)

# Have

E P I U+ **Have got**

▶ In pairs, ask and answer questions using *have got* and these words, e.g.

A – *Have you got any CDs?*
B – *Yes, I have. / No, I haven't.*
A – *What CDs have you got?*
B – *I've got ...*

> qualifications, brothers, scars, pets, children, books, toys, house plants, middle names, friends in London, relatives in the USA, English books

(Allocate one thing to each student to mingle and find out who in class has got the most qualifications, pets, etc.)

▶ In pairs, tell each other about the rooms and features your house has got, e.g. *My place has got a large, sunny kitchen.* Do the same for your country, e.g. *My country has got some of the most beautiful mountains in the world.*

E P I U+ **Have/Get something done**

▶ In small groups, tell each other about some things you've had done recently. Use these words, e.g. dentist – *I went to the dentist last week to have/get a tooth taken out.*

> garage, tailor, vet, dry cleaner, barber, printer's, hospital, photographer's

▶ Work in small groups. Imagine you have moved into a house which needs a lot of work doing to it. The renovation is half finished. Write two lists: things that you have had done and things that you are going to get done, e.g. *We've had the floorboards replaced. We're going to get a new bathroom put in upstairs.*

# Infinitive

E P I U+ **Purpose**

▶ Work in pairs. I'm going to say the names of some places. Take turns to ask and answer the question *Why did you go?*, e.g. T – *Bank.* A – *Why did you go to the bank?* B – *I went there to cash a cheque.*

> theatre, station, DIY shop, cinema, café, bakery, chemist, travel agent, post office

Write a list of five places you have been to in the last few days. Swap it with your partner and ask and answer the question *Why did you go?*

▶ I'm going to dictate the beginning of ten sentences. Write them down and add an ending.

> I'm going to save up to ...     I rang the theatre to ...
> I came to England to ...     He made a special cake to ...
> We stopped in Paris to ...     I'm studying English to ...
> I left home to ...     I went to Spain to ...
> I bought a bicycle to ...     She called me to ...

Compare your sentences with a partner.

## Why bother?

▶ In pairs, think of reasons for doing these things, e.g. write – *We write to tell one another our news.*

> study, drink coffee, run, think, breathe, cook, sleep, work, go to the gym, sigh, have children, learn English, eat, play the lottery, have showers

▶ In pairs, think of three activities. Write a sentence about each one explaining why you do it. Read out the reason for the class to guess the activity, e.g. *I do this to relax after a hard day at the office* (have a bath).

## Verb + infinitive

▶ In pairs, give each other instructions using this table, e.g. *I want you to speak more quietly.*

| I | want(s) | me | to | speak |
| You | would like | you | | help |
| He | need(s) | him | | go |
| She | don't want | her | | write |
| We | | us | | listen |
| They | | them | | look |

(Afterwards, elicit some reports, e.g. *I asked/told Tomas to speak more quietly.*)

▶ In pairs, ask and answer questions about the last time you did these things. Use the pattern verb + infinitive, e.g. *I promised to phone my brother more often.*

> agree, offer, decide, help, refuse, learn, promise, manage, hope, fail

## Like

## Like and would like

▶ In pairs, take it in turns to offer help with these problems, e.g. A – *I'm thirsty.* B – *Would you like a drink?*

> It's cold. I'm lost. My tea's cold. I'm hungry. My bags are heavy. I can't see properly. This is too spicy. I'm late for work. There's too much to do. I've got a headache.

▶ I'm going to read out some expressions. Write them under two headings: *Do you like ...?* and *Would you like ...?*

> a cup of tea, tea, speaking English, to speak English, cats, a cat, him, him to help, carrots, some more carrots, to meet Madonna, Madonna, going to the cinema, to go to the cinema, being a student, to be a student, flying, to fly there

In pairs, ask and answer similar questions, e.g.

A – *Do you like cats?*
B – *Yes, I do.*
A – *Would you like one of our kittens?*
B – *No thanks.*

## What's it like?

► In pairs, ask and answer questions about a country or city you know well, e.g.

A – *What are the trains like?*
B – *They're fast and efficient.*
A – *What's the coffee like?*
B – *It's strong.*

Here are some topics to help you.

| food, music, beaches, buses, people, flowers, weather, theatre, sports facilities, shops |
| --- |

► In small groups, ask and answer these questions, e.g.

A – *What's your boss like?*
B – *He's nice most of the time.*
A – *What does your boss like?*
B – *He likes keeping fit.*

| What | is<br>does | your | mother<br>father<br>teacher<br>best friend<br>boss | like? |
| --- | --- | --- | --- | --- |

► I'm going to give you lots of answers to these four questions.

| 1 What's ... like?  2 What does ... look like?  3 What does ... like?  4 How is ...? |
| --- |

Listen to the answers and shout out the right question, e.g. T – *He's angry.* S – *How is he?*

| He's happy. | Rachel likes dancing. | It's very beautiful. |
| --- | --- | --- |
| His dog is black. | It's always sunny. | Irene's exhausted. |
| Michael likes music. | She's glad. | The boy is thin. |
| The boy is hungry. | They like pizza. | He's got grey hair. |
| Scotland is cold. | Sheila's getting better. | It's raining outside. |

► In pairs, ask and answer questions about these animals, e.g.

A – *What do dogs like?*
B – *They like bones.*
A – *What are dogs like?*
B – *They're furry, loyal ...*

| monkeys, whales, cats, mice, snakes, rabbits, cows, dinosaurs, flies, spiders, elephants, birds, sharks |
| --- |

## Similes

In small groups, think of a short anecdote leading up to one of these similes. (Allocate one to each group, randomly chosen, without the other groups hearing. While they are working, write the similes on the board.) Read your anecdote to the class and see if they can guess which simile completes it.

| The next day he felt like death warmed up. | I felt like a fish out of water. |
| --- | --- |
| Well, you know me – I'm like a rolling stone. | Oh well – like father, like son I suppose. |
| It was like getting blood out of a stone. | He was like a bull in a china shop. |

## Like and as if

Work in small groups. Use these prompts to write two sentences for each, one with *like* and one with *as if*, e.g. He looks … – 1) *He looks like someone I used to know.* 2) *He looks as if he hasn't slept for a week.*

| | | |
|---|---|---|
| You look … | It feels … | Your job sounds … |
| My head feels … | Her flat looked … | Their baby looks … |
| This coffee tastes … | It sounds … | They seem … |
| The film sounds … | That man looks … | The food tasted … |
| His hair looked … | The town seemed … | Kevin's car sounds … |

## Passive

### Processes

► Listen to these questions and note down the key words. In pairs, answer the questions about a country you know well.

| | |
|---|---|
| What raw materials are produced? | What is exported and imported? |
| What is manufactured? | How are politicians elected? |
| What alcohol is made? | Which sports are played? |
| What is done with the rubbish? | How is electricity generated? |

► What's the relationship between these pairs of words?

grapes/wine, wheat/bread, tree/book, sheep/jumper, iron ore/spoon

In groups, choose a pair of words and list the stages of the process that makes one into the other, e.g. cacao/chocolate – *The cacao seeds are picked and dried. The seeds are shipped to the factory. At the factory, they are roasted. After roasting, the seeds are crushed. The pieces are ground into a fine paste. Cocoa powder and sugar are added. The resulting mixture is ground until it's smooth. The chocolate is poured into moulds. These are chilled to create chocolate.*

► Tell me how you were processed when you came to enrol at this school, e.g. *I was directed to reception where I was given a form to fill in. Then …*

### Famous people

In two groups, write sentences in the passive for the following, then three other sentences about famous people. When you have finished, test the other group, e.g. *It was discovered by Marie Curie* (radioactivity).

Don Quixote, psychoanalysis, $E = MC^2$, Mona Lisa, television, dynamite, Swan Lake, penicillin, Das Kapital, gravity, the telephone, Star Wars, evolution, printing

### What happened?

I'm going to ask you some questions. React as spontaneously as you can using the passive, e.g. T – *What happened to your hand?* S – *Oh, I was bitten by a dog.* (Ask each question to individuals at random. If the student stalls, invite answers from the whole class.)

| | |
|---|---|
| What happened to your arm? | Where's your bag? |
| Why aren't you riding your bike? | Where's your dog? |
| What happened to your leg? | Why are you late? |
| Why are you looking so disappointed? | What's wrong? |

**Newspaper headlines**

Work in small groups. Write these newspaper headlines as full sentences. (Allocate a few headlines to each group.) Continue the stories to make a complete news bulletin, e.g. Oil discovered in city centre – *Massive reserves of crude oil were discovered in the city centre yesterday when builders started digging the foundations for a new office block ...*

| | |
|---|---|
| Mobiles banned in class | Whale seen in Thames |
| Trapped girl saved | Titanic to be raised |
| Man abducted by aliens | Dog taught to drive |
| Robbers thwarted by OAP | Aussies beaten – at last |
| Woman hit by comet | Cure for cancer |

**Modernization**

▶ Imagine you arrive back in your home town after some time away and you discover tha the local government has made a lot of changes. Work in small groups and write passive sentences to describe these changes, e.g. *A brand new shopping and cinema complex has been built on the site of the old skating rink. All the factories have been demolished and the river is bein cleaned up to encourage tourists.*

(This activity is also good for the past perfect, if the return home was in the past, e.g. *The l time I went back to my city a lot of changes had been made ...*)

▶ In groups, discuss some of the changes that should be made to the area you live in, e.g. *The main road should be made into a pedestrian zone. That old building on the corner should be pulled down.*

In your groups, discuss some changes you think should be made to this school and/or classroom.

## Past continuous

**Fishy stories**

▶ In small groups, ask each other what you were doing yesterday at these times. In your answers, tell two lies. See if the group can identify which answers are lies.

05:00, 09:45, 12:00, 16:10, 19:15, 10:30

▶ In groups, brainstorm some very unlikely activities, write them on small pieces of paper and collect them into a pile, face down. Swap piles with another group.

(If any group is having difficulty coming up with ideas, add a few of these to their pile.)

catching a large fish, saving someone's life, snake charming, bungee jumping, hitch-hiking, sailing across the ocean, robbing a bank, riding a cow, darning socks, having an operation, swimming with sharks, having lunch with the US President

Take turns to pick a piece of paper from the pile, and explain to the group that you were doing the activity on the piece of paper at 7a.m. yesterday. Answer their questions, e.g.

A – *At 7 a.m. yesterday morning, I was flying in a balloon.*
B – *Why were you flying a balloon?*
A – *Because I was doing a scientific experiment.*
C – *Ah, and who was steering it?*
A – *Oh, there was a pilot ...*

## Setting the scene

► Here are the first lines of five stories. Write a few more sentences to set the scene, e.g. *The birds were singing and a lovely breeze was blowing off the lake. John was sitting on the jetty fishing. He was thinking about …*

> When we left the hotel it was a fine evening …
> The office was in a terrible state this morning …
> When I arrived the party had already started …
> It was a beautiful spring morning …
> I only left the kids for a minute and when I got back …

In small groups, read each other's ideas. Choose the best one and develop the story further. Delegate one person to do the writing. Choose someone to read the story out to the rest of the class.

► In pairs, discuss what was happening when …

> … you came into class.           … you last went into work.
> … you arrived at school.         … you got home yesterday.
> … you last switched on the TV.   … you went out this morning.

## Alibis

Last night at about 7.45 p.m. there was a murder. Two of you are suspects. (Choose two students.) Go outside the classroom and agree the details of everything you did yesterday evening from 7.15 to 8.15 p.m.

The rest of the class, you are investigators. Work in two groups and prepare a list of questions about what the suspects were doing at 7.45 p.m. Try to think of every detail. For example, if they went to a restaurant, where did they sit, what did they talk about, what was the waitress wearing?

Each group, interrogate one of the suspects. When you have finished, swap suspects and repeat your questions to the other one. Make a note of any differences you notice between the two stories. At the end report back to the class. What differences did you find? Are they guilty or not guilty?

## Past continuous and simple

## Newspaper headlines

Work in pairs. Write a few sentences about these headlines. Include information about what was happening when the event took place, e.g. Hikers stranded in snowstorm. – *A search and rescue team took nine hours to find a French couple yesterday, after a freak snowstorm hit the Pyrenees. Anton and Agathe Duval were hiking on the highest peak when the blizzard struck …*

> MP collapses at conference        Robbers caught during raid
> Lights go out at opening ceremony  Road rage in motorway jam
> Man eaten by pet alligator        Jogger mauled by dog
> Near miss at airport              Shopper sees Elvis

In your pairs, write a headline of your own, if possible about a story in the news at the moment. Pass it to the next pair and see if you can expand on the headline that is passed to you. I'll collect them in and read them out as a news bulletin.

**What next?**

Work in two groups. Write fifteen nouns on separate pieces of paper. Put them face down in the middle of the other group.

Take turns to choose a piece of paper and use the word to make a sentence about what you were doing when something else happened. Answer a question from the group about what you did next, e.g. TV.

A – *I was watching TV when the phone rang.*
B – *What did you do when the phone rang?*
A – *When the phone rang, I answered it.*

**Lifelines**

Look at the lifeline. In pairs, write a few sentences with *while* and *when* making up any details as necessary, e.g. *While he was living in Macau, he had an operation for ..., When his parents divorced, he moved to England with his ... because ... .*

| Born in Macau 1970 | Moved to UK 1978 | University 89–93 | Travelled 94–96 | Worked in bank 97–98 | Returned to London 1999 |
|---|---|---|---|---|---|
| Hospital operation 1974. Parents divorced 1977. | Secondary school 1981. Started guitar lessons. | Met girlfriend 1991. Went to Peru on holiday. | Married 1995. Accident in Namibia 1996. | Learnt French. Baby Rianne born 1997. Formed band. | First hit record 2000. Bought a mansion 2002. |

Draw your own lifeline. Exchange it with another student. Ask each other for more information and write similar sentences.

**Accident report**

► I'm going to dictate a description of an accident.

> Yesterday morning at 8.30 there was an accident between a bicycle and a lorry at the junction of Green Lanes and Seven Sisters Road. It was raining, but visibility was good. The lorry was travelling up Green Lanes and the cyclist was travelling west. Neither the lorry driver nor the cyclist was injured, but the bicycle was a mangled wreck. The driver and the cyclist both have to make a report to the police, which will be used in an insurance claim. They blame each other. There are some independent witnesses.

Work in groups of four to role-play the ensuing argument. (Add other roles if there are spare students in one group, e.g. the lorry driver's mate.)

Student A, you are the lorry driver.
Student B, you are the cyclist.
Student C, you are a witness.
Student D, you are a police officer. Ask questions.

When you have finished, write a report of what happened, from your point of view. Include information/questions about the traffic, the location, speed and direction of the vehicles and what you heard and saw next. Take turns to read out your report.

► In groups, tell each other about an accident you have been involved in, or witnessed.

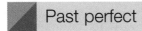

## Past perfect

### When

Work in pairs. Join a sentence from the first column with one from the second to make longer sentences, using *when*, e.g. The guests left. We tidied up. – *When the guests had left, we tidied up.* (Re-order the sentences in the second box when you write them up; they appear in the correct order here.)

| | |
|---|---|
| We unpacked our bags.<br>I read the book.<br>They signed the contract.<br>The baby fell asleep.<br>Oliver had a shower.<br>Rachael finished her pizza.<br>They tidied everything up.<br>They inspected his passport.<br>It stopped snowing.<br>She calmed down. | We went out.<br>I lent it to Tom.<br>They had a drink.<br>They went downstairs.<br>He felt better.<br>She asked for some coffee.<br>They went out.<br>He was free to go.<br>We continued our journey.<br>She explained the problem. |

### Arriving late

Work in pairs. I'm going to dictate the beginnings of some sentences. Write them down and decide how to finish them, e.g. When we finally got to the station – *the train had already left.*

| | |
|---|---|
| When we got to the theatre ...<br>When he got to the meeting ...<br>When I phoned for the job ... | By the time we arrived ...<br>When I switched on the TV ...<br>By the time she finally got up ... |

Write two more sentence beginnings and swap them with another pair. Write the endings for the sentences you receive and pass them back. Add another clause to the sentences you receive to explain what happened next, e.g. When we finally got to the station / *the train had already left / so we decided to go by coach.*

Read out the first two parts and see if anyone in class can guess what happened next.

### Prior events

I'm going to ask you ten questions. Write them down. In small groups, make up answers for them, e.g. T – *Why was Daniel so happy?* S – *Because he had recently been promoted.*

(Choose groups to read out their answers to the class at random and see if anyone can guess the question.)

| | |
|---|---|
| Why did Rachel feel sick?<br>Why was Jackie so miserable?<br>What did Tom find out when he phoned?<br>How was he different next time you saw him?<br>Where was his sandwich? | What did I realise when I got home?<br>Why was Ken so ecstatic?<br>Why was the office empty?<br>How much food was left?<br>Why did he feel so guilty? |

### Experiences

On your own, think back to a time when you went somewhere new and had a lot of new experiences. Make some notes, e.g. *Greece – moussaka.* Tell us about your experiences, e.g. *I had never eaten moussaka before I went to Greece.* (After a few sentences in open class, let students continue exchanging experiences together in pairs or small groups.)

**Preparations and changes**

▶ Work in small groups. Read these situations and think of ways to continue the narrative. Choose a secretary to write your ideas down, e.g. *When I visited my family, everything was different … My mum had thrown out the furniture in the sitting room. She had replaced the carpet with marble effect lino. She had painted the walls blue and brown. The kitchen was a disaster.*

| |
|---|
| 1  Josephine was about to arrive for dinner. Everything was ready … |
| 2  We were ready for our holiday … |
| 3  The Robertsons were coming to view the house, but it was still in a dreadful mess from the party … |
| 4  She wondered if all the preparations for the wedding were in place … |
| 5  When the ship arrived back in port, the whole town was waiting for them … |
| 6  He seemed quite comfortable when we discovered him on the desert island … |
| 7  By the time the cavalry arrived to save the town, it was too late … |
| 8  He had arrived in the future, but he didn't know exactly what year. Certainly, the world looked very different … |

▶ On your own, write a few sentences about a place or person you visited after a long time. Describe what changes had happened, e.g. *When I visited my old school they had built a new science block. The English teacher had taken over as headmaster.*

In small groups, ask and answer questions about the changes you wrote about. (Ask the students to put away their writing so that they are speaking rather than reading.)

**Explanations**

In pairs, imagine you saw your partner doing something interesting yesterday. Take turns to ask and answer questions to find out more, e.g.

A – *I saw you yesterday afternoon. Why were you staggering?*
B – *I was staggering because I had just walked into a lamp post and had concussion.*

| |
|---|
| crying, being arrested, covered in paint, wearing a wet suit, laughing, running after a mule, sleeping on a bench, carrying a sink, climbing a tree |

 Past simple

**Alphabet game**

In groups of three or four, take turns to use the past simple in a sentence. The first letter of the verbs must follow the sequence of the alphabet. If you can't think of one, you are out of the game. The next student continues with the next letter, e.g.

A – *He **a**sked me my name.* B – *I **b**ought a hat.* C – *I **c**ame here last month.*

(Variation: For higher levels, require that the sentences form a single narrative.)

**Yesterday**

Think of something you did yesterday and the time you did it, e.g. *Breakfast – 10 a.m.* Go round the class and find someone who did the same thing as you at approximately the same time, e.g.

A – *What time did you have breakfast yesterday?*
B – *I had breakfast at about 9.30.*

**Sequences**

Ask me some questions about what I did using these time expressions, e.g. S – *What did you do last night?* T – *I went home and had dinner. I watched the news and …*

| last night/week/year | this morning |
|---|---|
| in 1997 | the day before yesterday |
| on Tuesday / Sunday / New Year's Eve | three months ago |

(Write up one of your answers and add sequence markers, e.g. T – **First** *I went home and had a dinner.* **Then** *I watched the news and* **after that** *I … .*)

In pairs, ask and answer questions in the same way. Give a sequence of at least three things. (When everybody has finished, ask some students to report back to the class about their partners.)

**Substitutions**

Take turns to repeat this sentence, but substitute the word I write on the board, e.g. *It was very expensive.* (Write 'good'.) A – *It was very good.* (Write 'life'.) B – *Life was very good.*

1 I drove to the pub with him. (park, them, walked, her, shop, went, we, for, food)
2 This morning I washed the dishes. (he, car, afternoon, drove, she, her, lorry, crashed, my)
3 Last week I played football with Val. (we, Sunday, them, basketball, against, cricket, year, with)
4 I met my wife in 1980. (husband, 1997, friend, visited, we, September, they, arrested)
5 I didn't feel very well. (play, we, long, couldn't, much, see, they, clearly, think)
6 We had roast chicken for dinner. (boiled, potatoes, cold, breakfast, ate, they, mashed, made, us)

**Story chain**

Take turns to repeat what happened yesterday, and add something new, including a verb. If you forget the sequence, you are out of the game, e.g.

T – *Yesterday I found a €10 note in my pocket.*
A – *Yesterday I found a €10 note in my pocket and I bought a sandwich.*
B – *Yesterday I found a €10 note in my pocket and I bought a sandwich. I ate it.*
C – *Yesterday I found a €10 note in my pocket and I bought a sandwich. I ate it, and then I caught a train to Oxford.*

(Restart the activity when the sequence gets too long.)

(Variation: Restrict the activity to irregular verbs. For higher levels, ask students to choose their verbs before the game begins.)

**Whispers**

I'm going to whisper a sentence to someone. This student has to whisper the same sentence to the person next in line. The last student will say the sentence aloud to the class and I'll write it on the board. I'll then tell you the sentence we started with. (This works best if the students are sitting or standing in a circle.)

| We met Samantha and Raymond at Pizza Pasta on the corner of Old Street and shared a Four Seasons pizza and a bottle of wine. |
|---|

Write your own sentence, including at least two irregular pasts. Sit in a circle and send your messages round the class in the same direction. Write down the sentence as it gets back to you. Read it out and read out the original sentence. How many differences are there between the two sentences?

**I don't believe you**

Work in small groups. Take turns to tell the group what you did yesterday. The group will interrupt you after every two or three sentences with *I don't believe you!* Change your last sentence and continue the story, e.g.

A – *I got up at 7.30 and had a shower ...*
Group – *I don't believe you!*
A – *I got up at 7.30 and had a cigarette. Then I went out for breakfast. I read the paper and ...*
Group – *I don't believe you!*
A – *I read my letters and then I caught the bus to work. I arrived at 9 a.m. ...*

**The first time**

In pairs, tell each other about your first:

> bicycle, pet, job, friend, home, toys, swim, holiday, memory, day at school, alcoholic drink, word (as a baby), car, flight in a plane

**The last time**

► Work in pairs. Ask each other questions about the last time you did these things, e.g. A – *When did you last go to the cinema?* B – *The last time I went to the cinema was two weeks ago. I saw ...*

> eat an egg, take exercise, shake hands, travel by boat, have a cold, cook a meal, laugh, feel sad, wear a suit, have a dance, send an e-mail, break something valuable, clean the windows, tell a lie, stay up all night

► In pairs, ask and answer questions beginning *What was the last time you ...?* After each answer, ask another question, e.g. A – *What was the last thing you sold?* B – *An old camera.* A – *How much did you sell it for?* B – *I sold it for € 25.*

> buy, make, break, eat, sell, write, drink, learn, find, read, dream about, throw away

**First and last times**

Work in two teams. Write twenty infinitive verbs on pieces of paper. Put them face down in a pile in the middle of the other team. Take turns to pick up a verb and make a sentence with it, beginning *The first time I ...* or *The last time I ...*

If your sentence is correct, your team keeps the verb. If the other team spots a mistake and challenges you, they get the verb. The winning team is the one with the most verbs.

**Matthew's day**

In pairs, put these phrases in the past and arrange them in a reasonable order to talk about Matthew's day. Join them using *and, then* and *after that,* plus any other words you think are necessary.

> go downstairs, get in car, have shower, take dog for walk, go outside, drive to work, let cat in, wake up kids, get up, buy milk, read paper, wake up, make tea

Write a question about each sentence, e.g. *What time did he get up?*

Join another pair to ask and answer your questions. As a group of four, continue the story of his day. Choose someone to read it out to the class, e.g. *When he got to work, he read his e-mails. Then he ...*

## Reactions

I'm going to dictate eight pairs of short sentences. Write them down, leaving a space after each pair.

1  She reads the letter. She throws it in the bin.
2  The shark appears. They panic.
3  He looks in the cupboard. He sees a mouse.
4  The mouse sees him. It runs away.
5  The bell rings. They run out into the playground.
6  They try my curry. Everyone starts choking.
7  The rain stops. We go out to play frisbee.
8  I get home. I switch on the radio.

Join each pair of sentences to make one sentence in the past, beginning with *when*, e.g. *When she heard the baby cry, she went to feed him.*

On your own, write a few pairs of sentences about things you have done in the last few days. Swap your pairs of sentences with a partner. Join the ones you receive in the same way and pass them back.

## Possessive adjectives and pronouns

### Possessiveness

Listen to these sentences and shout out another, using a possessive pronoun instead of the possessive adjective, e.g. *It's my book.* – *The book is mine.*

| | | |
|---|---|---|
| It's my pen. | It's your car. | This is his house. |
| It's her jumper. | This is our garden. | That's their dog. |
| That's my bag. | It's their baby. | That is my man. |

In pairs, see if you can write all nine pairs of sentences from memory.

### Bucket pronouns

(Collect small objects from the students and put them in a cardboard box or bag. Take an object out and elicit this sequence.)

T – Is this yours?
A – No, it's not mine.
T – Whose is it then?
A – It's his/hers/Maria's, etc.

(Write the exchange on the board. Walk around the class inviting students to take an object and have a similar exchange with their partner. Gradually erase the model from the board.)

### What about yours?

In pairs, change the noun and adjective in this question to make five more questions.

My shoes are brown; what about yours?

With a new partner, take turns to ask and answer your questions.

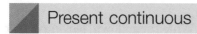

## Present continuous

`E P I U+` ### What's happening?

I'm going to dictate the beginnings of some sentences. Write them down. In pairs, think of suitable endings using the present continuous, e.g. *Please turn the TV off; I'm trying to study.*

| | |
|---|---|
| Don't disturb me; I'm ... | Drink your tea; it's ... |
| Don't listen to him; he's ... | Leave the radio on; I'm ... |
| Quick! Pass the spanner; I'm ... | Look at that man; he's ... |
| I can't see you right now; I'm ... | Shhh! Listen. That man's ... |

Think of two similar sentences that would be useful to you, e.g. *Pass me the calculator; I'm working out my share of the household bills.*

`E P I U+` ### Houses and rooms

(Draw the cross section of a large house on the board, with at least eight rooms over three floors.)

Which rooms are which? (Elicit ideas and label the rooms.)

Who lives here? (Elicit some names and their relationships.)

In small groups, imagine it's 8.00 p.m. and everyone is at home. Agree where they are and what they're doing, e.g. *Lorraine is listening to very loud music in her bedroom. John, her dad, i in the hall shouting, 'Turn it down.'*

Think about your family and friends. Discuss what you think they're doing right now.

`E P I U+` ### Clothes

(Ask a student what he/she wears or is wearing, and then to repeat the question to anothe student, e.g.

T – *Manuel, are you wearing jeans?*
Manuel – *No, I'm not. Are you wearing jeans, Ilona?*
Ilona – *Yes, I am.*
T – *Brigit, do you wear a scarf?*
Brigit – *Yes, I do, during the winter. Do you wear a scarf, Peter?*)

`E P I U+` ### Mimes  ⚠

Guess what I am doing. (Mime these activities.)

flying a kite, washing a glass, driving a fast car, watching tennis,
eating a fish, brushing a cat, having a tooth out, feeding a lion, drinking wine,
watching football on TV, doing brain surgery, doing sums, looking at the moon,
changing a nappy, catching a butterfly, listening to reggae, eating a boiled egg

Work in two teams. Take turns to mime a continuous action for your group to guess. Score a point if they can guess your mime within thirty seconds.

`E P I U+` ### The world outside

(With classes taking place in busy locations such as a city centre, open the windows. Ask the students to keep quiet for a few minutes and make a note of anything they hear going on outside, e.g. *A man is talking loudly on his mobile phone.* As a follow up, ask them to imagine they are in another location with lots of sounds and write a similar description, e.g. at the seaside, in a busy restaurant.)

## Wish you were here

In pairs, imagine you are on holiday in an idyllic location. You are sitting in a café and there's a lot going on, both inside and outside. Write a postcard to someone back home telling them what's happening around you. Include descriptions of the weather, the people you can see, the city/town, the food and drink, the hotel, and your arrangements for the next day.

## These days

► Imagine you find your diary from a few years ago. As you leaf through it, you find different entries beginning with the following sentences. Continue each entry, e.g.

Life is boring ... – *I'm studying every evening for my exam. Meanwhile all my mates are going out and enjoying themselves. Dominic's not talking to me any more either. I'm not having any fun at all!*

| | |
|---|---|
| Spring is here ... | I need a holiday ... |
| My new job is exciting ... | We don't get on any more ... |
| We're having a lovely time ... | Fiona sent us a letter ... |

Compare your ideas with a partner.

In pairs, tell each other what is happening in your life these days outside the classroom. Include information about the following.

| |
|---|
| family, accommodation, work, hobbies, studies, eating habits, routines |

► In two groups, discuss what's happening in the world these days. Include information about the following.

| |
|---|
| IT, the environment, life expectancy, sport, the (global) economy, culture/fashion |

Agree a list of the ten most important things. Compare your list with the other group.

## Future arrangements

Do you remember all your appointments or do you have to write them down in a dairy?

Copy this weekend planner and fill in any three spaces, leaving the others blank. Think of some unusual things to do, e.g. whale watching, skydiving. (Make sure the students only fill in three spaces.)

| | Saturday | Sunday |
|---|---|---|
| Morning | | |
| Afternoon | | |
| Evening | | |

Make arrangements with some other students for the remaining times in your diary, e.g.

A – *Are you doing anything on Saturday afternoon?*
B – *Yes. I'm having dinner with my agent.*
A – *Oh. What about Sunday evening?*
B – *Uhm ... No. I'm free then.*
A – *Would you like to come to the cinema?*
B – *OK. What do you want to see?*
A – *I've heard about this great film ...*

**Annoying habits**

▶ In pairs, think of someone you know with annoying habits. Tell your partner about him/her. Don't choose someone in the class! Give each other some advice about how to deal with the person, e.g.

A – *I hate him! He's always teasing me!*
B – *You should just ignore him.*

▶ I'm going to give you an adjective that describes a person. In pairs, write a sentence about this person's bad habits, e.g. anti-social – *He's always playing loud music until the early hours of the morning.* (Distribute the adjectives amongst the pairs. Allow the students to use dictionaries.)

---

argumentative, boring, bossy, careless, conceited, dirty, forgetful, greedy, grumpy, lazy, mean, moody, paranoid, selfish, unreliable, untidy, weird

---

Read out your sentence and see if anyone can guess the adjective.

**Project**

Before the next class, go to a place in this town where there are usually a lot of things happening. Write a description of everything you can see and hear. In class, read out your description. Can anyone guess where it is?

## Present perfect

**Past participles**

▶ In groups of four, make sentences using past participles in alphabetical order. If you can't think of one, you are out of the game, e.g.

A – *I've **a**nswered his letter.*
B – *He's **b**lown the whistle.*
C – *I've **c**ooked something special.*
D – *I've never **d**riven a car.*

▶ Work in two teams. I'm going to read a list of nouns. If you think you can use one in a present perfect sentence, put your hand up. If your sentence is correct, your team gets a point. If it's wrong, the other team gets a point, and another attempt with the same word e.g. tea – *I've made you some tea.*

---

cat, bags, dentist, hair, car, tree, shower, Roger, shirt, Wales, love, house, road, Janet, café, person, phone, map, dinner, rain, factory, light bulb, egg, nose, computer, duck

---

▶ In two teams, listen to these infinitives and shout out the past participle, If you're correct, your team gets a point. If you're wrong, the other team gets a point, and another attempt at the same verb.

---

bite, leave, hide, steal, swim, win, put, see, wear, eat, think, know, show, buy, be, throw, drink, sit, ring, stand, let, grow, lose, give, do, shut, teach, speak, run, make, catch, go, bring, ride, rise, tell, shine, sell, fly, take, get, come, keep, break, fight

---

▶ (Write some infinitives which have irregular past participles in a noughts and crosses grid.

Work in two teams to play noughts and crosses. Take turns to choose a square. To win it you have to tell me the past participle of the verb in the square and use it in a sentence.

## Life experience

Mingle and ask each other *Have you ever ...?* questions about these subjects. Make a note of who has done these things.

> crash/car, ride/horse, work/nights, swim/river, sing/public, go/diving,
> make/bread, win/prize, sleep/outside, catch/fish, wear/tie, break/bone,
> buy someone/flowers, eat/caviar, climb/mountain, do/bungee jump

## Tell me more

In pairs, ask and answer questions about whether you have ever done these things. If the answer is yes, find out some more information, e.g.

A – *Have you ever broken a bone?*
B – *Yes, I have.*
A – *When was that?*
B – *When I was at school.*
A – *What happened?*
B – *I broke my arm playing rugby.*

> cut your finger, eat Indian food, have an injection, see an eclipse,
> wear fancy dress, live by the sea, go on a demonstration,
> do anything brave, sleep in a tent, sail a boat, drive a tractor

Tell your partner something you've done which you don't think anyone else in class has done, and something you've never done which you think another student in class has done, e.g. I've been scuba diving. I've never played cricket, but I think Shaqil probably has.

Tell us what your partner said and find out if his/her guesses are true.

## A romantic dinner

Shout out some things you associate with a romantic dinner. (Write them up on the board.)

> wine, candles, soft music, best suit or dress, table,
> housework, roses, perfume/aftershave, chocolates

Imagine you are script writers for a soap opera. You are setting the scene for one of the female actors who has prepared a romantic dinner for her boyfriend. Tell me what she has done, using the words on the board, e.g. dinner – *She's cooked the dinner.*

There's a knock at the door. (Ask the students to guess who it is). It's her mother. She doesn't like her daughter's boyfriend. (Elicit ideas about why, e.g. *She wants her to marry someone from a rich family.*) The daughter doesn't want her mother to find out about the date. She is very suspicious and asks lots of questions.

In pairs, role-play the conversation, e.g.

Mum – *Why have you cooked dinner?*
Daughter – *Er ... because I'm hungry, Mum ...*
Mum – *But why have you cooked so much?*
Daughter – *Well, I thought you might turn up, Mum.*
Mum – *And why have you bought flowers?*

There is another knock at the door. This time it's her boyfriend.

In groups of three, role-play the conversation between the daughter, her mother and the boyfriend. (If male students in your class feel uncomfortable about playing a female role, change the role of the mother to her father.)

**Preparations**

In pairs, imagine you are going on holiday. Make a list of ten things that need to be done, e.g. book the hotel.

Now imagine you are about to leave and go to the airport. Take turns to ask each other questions, e.g.

A – *Have you packed the towels?*
B – *Yes, I have. Have you brought the passports?*
A – *Yes, I have. Have you ...?*

(Variation: Give different groups different tasks, e.g. preparations for a party, a wedding, a job interview or a date.)

**Changes**

► (Before break, draw a picture of a person on the board and elicit features, hairstyle, clothes, etc. During break, make some drastic changes.) In pairs, discuss what has happened to the person on the board, e.g *He's grown a beard. He's lost an eye.*

► In groups, discuss what changes have taken place in the world in the last 50 years. Here are some ideas to help you.

| computers, fashion, food, rich and poor, politics, work, medicine, music, TV, transport |

► In pairs, continue these conversations with an explanation using the present perfect and a follow-up question, e.g.

A – *Why are you limping?*
B – *I've been in a car accident.*
A – *Oh dear. How did that happen?*

| | |
|---|---|
| Why aren't you at work? | You seem so happy these days. Why is that? |
| Why have you packed your bags? | Long time no see. Where have you been? |
| What's happened to your hair?! | Is there something wrong? You look worried. |

**Time game**

Take turns to repeat this sentence, using the ending I give you and adding *for* or *since* as necessary, e.g.

T – *I've known him since March.*
A – *I've known him since March.*
T – *Two weeks.*
B – *I've known him for two weeks.*

| |
|---|
| I've been here ...<br>July, three days, 1998, ten years, yesterday, Christmas, five, minutes, ages,<br>Saturday, my whole life, August, an hour and a half, last weekend,<br>Monday, a while, almost a month<br><br>I've been waiting ...<br>an hour, eight o'clock, five minutes, Tuesday, two years, weeks, ages, we arrived,<br>June 2001, long enough, half an hour, the doors opened, nearly three months,<br>the beginning of term, last Wednesday, about ten minutes |

(Variation: Ask the students to run the drill in groups, with one person dictating the time expressions. Then ask the students to add another phrase, such as the thing they've been waiting for, e.g. *I've been waiting since January for a visa to visit Finland.*)

## For and since

► I'm going to ask someone a question. Answer it, and then ask someone else the same question. Repeat this pattern until I start a new question. There's one important rule. (Write *for* and *since* on the board.) Your answer must include *for* or *since*, depending on which word on the board I'm pointing at when you answer, e.g.

T – *How long have you been studying English, Ramon?*
Ramon – *I've been studying English for two years, part-time. Sara, how long have you been studying English?*
Sara – *I've been studying English since February last year.*

| | |
|---|---|
| How long have you known your teacher? | How long have you been living in ...? |
| How long have you been in this lesson? | How long have you been in this school? |
| How long have you been using this book? | How long have you been doing this activity? |

► What verbs go with these things? (Only accept these verbs. Write them on the board.)

English (study), bicycle (ride), house/flat (live), yellow socks (wear),
musical instrument (play), hobby (do), disco (go), boy/girlfriend (go out with),
football (play), credit card (use), book/novel (read), cigarettes (smoke)

Mingle and ask the other students how long they have been doing the things, e.g.

A – *Have you got a car?*
B – *Yes, I have.*
A – *How long have you been driving?*
B – *I've been driving since January / for six months.*

Try to find someone who does each thing. Make a note of their name and how long they have been doing it.

► Here's the beginning of a sentence. (Write *I haven't ...* on the board.) I'm going to give you ten endings. In pairs, complete the sentences, e.g. this morning. – *I haven't eaten since this morning.*

two hours, last term, ten o'clock, I came to England, three days,
I was at school, Sunday, ten years, a week, I was little, yesterday

Read your sentences out, stopping at *for* or *since* for the others to guess the ending.

## Still, yet, already and just

In pairs, write four endings for these sentences, using *still*, *yet*, *already* and *(only) just*, e.g.

He's been working here for a week ...
– *and he still hasn't met the boss.*
– *and he hasn't got a desk yet.*
– *and he's already got an office.*
– *and he's only just got a computer.*

Their baby is two and a half and he ...
Rob's been studying English for two months ...
I sent them the application last week and ...
It's 11.30 a.m. and ...
They've been married for six months ...
We've been on holiday for three days ...
She's been shopping all morning ...
I've been waiting for over an hour ...

Translate some of the sentences into your own language.

**Recent events**

▶ In small groups, think of a reason for these exclamations, e.g. Ouch! – *Someone has just stubbed their toe.*

> Sorry! What? Sorry? Never mind. OK, when? You're joking!
> No, thanks. Great! Wow! Really? Bad luck! Bless you!
> Well done! Help! Cheers! God! Of course. Uh-oh! So?

▶ I'm going to ask you why you're behaving strangely. Mime the behaviour, and explain using the present perfect, e.g. T – *Why are you so tired?* S – (stretching and yawning) *Because I've been working all night.*

> shivering, crying, so filthy, angry, so tired, laughing, eating so much,
> so excited, so bored, bleeding, limping, hiding under the desk, wet,
> not sitting on your chair, holding that baby, being so friendly, shouting

▶ In pairs, write suitable answers to these questions using the present perfect, e.g. *Why is it so hot in here? Because someone has left the heating on. / Because someone has been baking bread.*

> Why is it so cold in here? Why are the police here? What's in the news today?
> What's the matter? Where's my car? How's your family? What's that smell?

Compare your ideas with another pair.

(Variation: Ask the students to write the most unexpected answer they can think of. Then they work together in pairs to guess each other's answers.)

## Present simple

**Questions**

▶ In pairs, ask and answer questions, using this table to help. Make some notes.

| When<br>What time | do you<br>does he/she | get up<br>go to work<br>get home<br>have dinner<br>go to bed | on | Mondays?<br>Saturday mornings? |
|---|---|---|---|---|
| | | | in the | morning?<br>afternoon?<br>evening? |
| | | | at | night?<br>the weekend? |

Find a new partner. Ask and answer questions about the first partner, in the third person.

▶ In pairs, match a verb from the first column with a word from the second to make a phrase. (Re-order the words in the second box when you write them up; they appear here in the correct order.)

> live, drink, like, play, watch, go,
> ride, speak, read, drive, get up

> alone, tea with milk, dogs, chess, horror films, dancing,
> a bicycle, German, the Sunday papers, a car, early

Use the phrases to ask your partner questions. Give short answers, e.g. eat + beef. A – *Do you eat beef?* B – *Yes, I do. / No, I don't.*

## Regular events

► How often do you come to class? How often do you get up late? (Use similar questions to elicit these frequency expressions. Write them on the board.)

| once/twice three times | a | day week month year |
|---|---|---|
| once every | | three days every other day |

I'm going to give you each an activity. Mingle, and find out who does it the most and who does it the least. (After the survey, elicit the results and write them on the board.)

> buy new clothes, eat pasta, sleep in, drink tea, cook, get a haircut, dance, visit relatives, do the laundry, surf the Internet, use a drill, dream, do arithmetic, sing, eat out, read a book, go on holiday, tidy up, visit the dentist, fly, go to the park

► In small groups, discuss these topics.

> a typical weekend at home
> the people in your home town
> the main festivals in your home country

## Stories and jokes

► Think of a film or book that you really enjoyed. Spend a few minutes refreshing your memory and making some notes. In small groups, tell each other all about it, but don't tell them the title. See if anyone can guess from your description, e.g. *There's a boy called Harry, who has got magical powers. Unfortunately he lives with his horrible aunt and uncle, the Dursleys. They're 'muggles' – ordinary human beings ...*

► (Invite students to think of some jokes in English and tell the class in a later lesson, e.g. *There's this bloke who goes into a pub. He's got a mouse in his pocket ... .*)

## Itineraries

Work in pairs. Imagine you are PAs to a busy executive who has to attend a number of meetings in New York and Las Vegas next Monday and Tuesday. Write a detailed itinerary for the trip, including travel arrangements, meetings, hotels and entertainment. Make sure you both have a copy of the itinerary.

Swap partners and role-play this conversation.

Student A, you are the personal assistant.

Student B, you are the executive. You are putting some of the details into your personal organiser and you keep checking them. You also want to make time during the trip for some gambling and other things, e.g.

A – *You depart from Heathrow, Terminal 3 at 8.10 a.m., flight BA724.*
B – *Terminal 3 at 8.10. BA742.*
A – *No, it's flight BA724.*
B – *OK, 724. Is it an aisle seat?*
A – *Yes. You arrive at JFK at 9.20 local time.*
B – *Uh-huh. That's 21.20 local time.*
A – *No, you arrive in the morning ...*

When you have finished, swap roles.

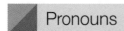

## Pronouns

### Personal pronouns

► (Write this table on the board, eliciting the pronouns as you do so.)

| I | love | me |
|---|---|---|
| you | like | you |
| he | hate | him |
| she | want | her |
| it | don't like | it |
| we | | us |
| they | | them |

Take turns to say a sentence and then a question using the words in the table, e.g.

A – *She likes him.*
B – *Why does she like him?*
C – *They don't like her.*
D – *Why don't they like her?*

► In small groups, take turns to say as many sentences as you can using these words, as quickly as possible, e.g. *He wants us to listen.*

| I | want(s) | me | to | speak |
|---|---|---|---|---|
| you | would like | you | | go |
| he | need(s) | him | | write |
| she | asked | her | | listen |
| we | told | it | | look |
| they | don't want | us | | |
| | | them | | |

Add another preposition, where possible, and another pronoun, e.g. *He wants us to listen to him.*

### Reflexive pronouns

► Use these pairs of words and a reflexive pronoun in sentences, e.g. matches/burn – *He burnt himself while he was playing with matches.*

> tea/make, present/buy, mirror/admire, sweets/sick, cake/help, pay rise/give, drink/pour, dinner/cook, gun/shoot, question/ask, card/send, help/more

Using some of the same verbs, make sentences that are true for you, and tell your partner, e.g. *I made myself a nice cup of coffee and watched TV.*

► In small groups, discuss these questions.

> When do you most enjoy yourself?
> What kind of things can switch themselves off?
> Are you sure of yourself?
> Tell us about a time when you really admired yourself.
> What do you say when you invite someone into your house?
> What does DIY mean? Are you any good at DIY?
> How often do you think about yourself?
> Name someone who takes himself/herself too seriously.
> Who in the group looks at himself/herself the most in the mirror?

## Quantifiers

P I U+

### Overview

In small groups, put these expressions into the table. Some go in more than one place.

> how many, a lot of, how much, there are, not many, not much,
> loads, a little, a few, any, some, enough, plenty, there is

|  | Countable | Uncountable |
|---|---|---|
| Positive |  |  |
| Question and Negative |  |  |

Think of an example for each one that's true for your group, e.g. *Olga has got lots of sisters.*
(Draw the table large on the board so there's plenty of room for examples.)

P I U+

### Tic-Tac-Toe

(Draw a noughts and crosses grid on the board with these words.) Work in two teams.
Play noughts and crosses. Take turns to choose a square. To win it, you have to make
a sentences with the words in the square.

> how much, a lot, plenty, some, not many, a little, a few, too much, any

In pairs, play the game again. If you think your opponent's sentence is wrong, ask me.

P I U+

### Countable and uncountable

▶ Work in small groups. Are these words countable or uncountable?

> news, meat, money, star, stairs, person, advice, equipment, politics, information

▶ Listen to these words and put them under three headings: countable, uncountable, or both.

> book, job, pepper, bread, energy, work, orange, sandwich, cake,
> furniture, snow, fish, literature, window, bottle, country, sleep, time,
> juice, mouse, glass, word, paper, table, question, salt, loaf, hair

Write two sentences using each of the words in the third column, once as a countable noun
and once as an uncountable noun, e.g. *I like stuffed red peppers. I always add lots of pepper to
my food.*

P I U+

### Geography game

Work in groups of three. Think of a country each, but don't tell the others what it is.
Ask each other quantity questions about these things to guess the country, e.g.

A – *Are there many skyscapers?*
B – *No, there aren't many. / Yes, there are a lot.*
A – *Is there much rain?*
B – *No there isn't much. / Yes, there's a lot.*

> mountains, wildlife, pyramids, skyscrapers, snow, crime, sand, traffic, camels,
> bicycles, religions, beaches, languages, fresh water, tourism, people, pollution

**My fridge**

▶ Take turns to repeat this sentence, but substitute the word I write on the board. (See Substitutions on page 93 for full instructions.)

> Is there much food in the fridge? (house, furniture, your, any, wine, the, fridge, fish, are, pond, many, river, sea)

▶ Ask me about the contents of my fridge, e.g. *How much milk have you got? How many egg have you got?* I will answer any correct questions in as much detail as I can. When you have asked a correct question do not ask any more until everyone has had a go.

Work in pairs and ask your partner about his/her fridge.

## Question forms

**Wh- and yes/no questions**

▶ Work in pairs. Copy the table and complete it by writing questions and answers.

| What<br>When<br>Who<br>Where<br>Why<br>Which<br>Whose<br>How | *What's he doing?* | *He's ironing.* | Do<br>Does<br>Did<br>Are<br>Is<br>Can<br>Would<br>Will | *Do you like me?* | *Yes, I do.* |
|---|---|---|---|---|---|
| | | | | | |

I will say a question word. Student A, you have five seconds to use it in a question to your partner. Student B, answer it. For the next question, it's Student B's turn, e.g.

T – *where*
A – *Where do you live?*
B – *I live in Madrid.*
T – *when*
B – *When is your birthday?*

▶ Work in two groups. Agree a list of the ten best questions to help you guess the identity of an object you can't see, e.g. *What's it made of? How big is it? Is it man-made?* The questions must start with one of the question words from the table. You can't ask what the object is called.

Find a partner from the other group. Take turns to think of an everyday object and use your ten questions to work out what it is. Which group's questions do you think are the most effective?

▶ Work in two teams to play noughts and crosses. (Draw a grid on the board with these words.) Take turns to choose a square. To win it, you have to make a question with the question words.

> when, why, who, where, how much, how, what, which, whose

(You can also play with yes/no questions: *do, can, is, will, have, are, did, was* and *would.*)

▶ Ask me as many questions as you can about my shoes, e.g. *Where did you buy them? How long have you had them? How often do you wear them?* In pairs, ask and answer similar questions. (This activity also works well with: flat, job, hair, etc.)

## Interviews ⚠

In pairs, ask questions to help you fill in this form with information about your partner, e.g. *What's your name?*

| | |
|---|---|
| Name _____ | Age _____ |
| Address _____ | Nationality_____ |
| _____ | Marital Status _____ |
| _____ | Children _____ |
| Telephone number _____ | Job _____ |

Keep your notes and swap partners. Ask and answer questions about the person on your partner's form, e.g. *What's her name?*

## Reply questions

I'm going to tell you something to reply to with a short question, e.g.

T – *It's raining.* S – *Is it?* T – *Yes, it is.*
T – *It's not here.* S – *Isn't it?* T – *No, it isn't.*

(Model the rising intonation of the question, then choose students at random.)

| | |
|---|---|
| He's just arrived. | She wasn't there. |
| I'm studying economics. | Look. Harry gave me this. |
| There's an e-mail for you. | He's not in. |
| I'd like to try. | You look ill. |
| I passed! | Ron's got yours. |
| We've run out of sugar. | Glenda won't like it. |
| We're going. | There's no one at home. |
| I'll be back late. | You should go. |
| They had a fight. | You're late! |
| I don't know. | I'm pregnant again. |
| We've moved to Belgium. | The lights don't work. |
| Nobody came to the party. | We'd better not tell. |

In groups of three, take it in turns to say a statement to the student on your left to reply to with a short question.

(Variation: Get students to add surprise/disappointment when replying to positive statements, e.g. *A – It's snowing. B – It isn't, is it?* Model the intonation.)

## Questionnaires

In groups of five, write a questionnaire with five questions about the topic I give you. Make sure you all have a copy of the questions, e.g. 1) *Do you own a computer?* 2) *How long do you spend on line every day?*

| |
|---|
| computers, music, the environment, food leisure |

(Number the students from one to five within each group, and ask them to form new groups of students with the same number – all the 1s together, all the 2s together, etc.)

In your new groups, ask and answer your questions and write a report of your findings in 100 words, e.g. *Half the students in the group own a computer. They spend an average of 45 minutes a day on line ...*

**Indirect questions**

► Work in pairs. I'm going to read out twelve sentences. Eight have mistakes and four are correct. Write them down, correcting the mistakes.

> 1  Do you know what time does the train arrive?
> 2  Tell me what is the problem.
> 3  Can you tell me where is East Street?
> 4  Could you let us know when he arrives?
> 5  Do you know if this is the way to the station?
> 6  I'd like to know where is the library?
> 7  Could you let us know are you coming?
> 8  Do you understand what are they saying?
> 9  Please tell me who's in charge.
> 10  I wonder will it be sunny tomorrow.
> 11  I'm trying to find out how much was my last bill.
> 12  Can you tell me where the buffet car is?

► In pairs, write eight indirect questions about your English lessons, e.g. *I'd like to know when the holiday begins. Could you tell me when the next vocabulary test is?*

**Questions for answers**

► (Write up ten answers about yourself.) Here are some answers to questions about me. What were the questions? e.g.

Scotland – *Where were you born?*
Two of each – *How many brothers and sisters have you got?*
When I was five – *When did you start school?*

Write a list of five answers about yourself. Swap lists with a partner and work out the questions.

► Work in two teams. I'm going to give you some answers. If you can think of the question, put your hand up. Your team gets one point for each reasonable question.

> No, never.  Next week.  Yesterday.  Since yesterday.  Of course!  Not bad.  €10.
> Sorry?  5.30 a.m.  By train.  On Friday.  Not many.  On Fridays.  In the kitchen.
> Yes, you are.  A Mercedes.  We had a curry.  OK, fine.  No, thanks.  Gardening.

**Yes/No Game**

Work in pairs. Student A, try to get student B to say yes or no by quickly asking twenty questions. If he/she says yes or no, you win. If you run out of questions, he/she wins. Then swap roles, e.g. A – *Do you smoke?* B – *Never!* A – *Would you like to try one?* B – *I'd rather not, thanks.* A – *But I saw you smoking yesterday.* B – *No, you didn't!* (B loses because he/she said no.)

**Questions for questions**

Work in pairs and write a short conversation using only questions, e.g. A – *Are you OK?* B – *Why are you asking?* A – *Do you have to be so defensive?* B – *What makes you think I'm defensive?*

Compare your conversation with another pair. (Invite the pairs to read out their conversation to the class.)

## Question tags

P | I | U+

### Making sure

(Write *We've never met before, …* on the board and ask students to tell you the question tag. Model the pronunciation for this question: 1) for a real question, with a rising intonation; and 2) a request for confirmation, with a falling intonation. Elicit situations in which each question could be asked.)

Take turns to read out one of these sentences, adding a question tag. Decide whether you want it to be: 1) a real question, or 2) a request for confirmation. I'll say 1 or 2 depending on what I hear.

| | | |
|---|---|---|
| It's a lovely day. | He didn't say that. | You've got my dictionary. |
| The exam's on Wednesday. | Ben's really full of himself. | Kate's beautiful. |
| We've never met before. | There aren't any left. | You've finished now. |
| You don't like me. | This is absolutely rubbish. | That isn't Elvis Presley. |
| You don't agree. | I'll see you again. | Something's wrong. |

In pairs, choose some of the questions and write short dialogues, e.g.

A – *You know Stan, don't you?*
B – *No, I don't think I've ever met him.*
A – *Are you sure? Weren't you at Jane's party last month? He was the DJ.*
B – *Oh, that's Stan. Yes, I know him!*

P | I | U+

### Making conversation

In pairs, look at this conversation. Where do you think the conversation is happening? Read it out between you, adding a question tag in each gap. (When the students have finished ask for two volunteers to read it out to the class.)

> A – This is great, _____ ?
> B – Yes, it is. And there's plenty of food, _____ ?
> A – Absolutely. The bride looks stunning, _____ ?
> B – I know, and her new husband's so handsome, _____ ?
> A – Yes, but he doesn't say much, _____ ?
> B – No, he can't speak very good English, _____ ?
> A – Hmm.... That's not Roger, _____ ?
> B – Oh yes. He's got a bit fat, _____ ?
> A – You're telling me. That can't be his new partner, _____ ?
> B – I'm not sure. Let's find out, _____ ?

(Variation: Dictate the sentences and students add the question tags afterwards.)

In the same pairs, write a similar conversation for one of the following situations. (Elicit the ideas in brackets that follow each situation. Let students choose which situation they want, but ensure that each situation is covered by at least one pair.)

> 1 in a restaurant, after a nice meal (opinions about the food, the decor, the service, the bill, etc.)
> 2 leaving to go on holiday (checking that everything is ready: packing, tickets, etc.)
> 3 on holiday, having a walk (the weather, the people, the holiday so far, etc.)
> 4 talking about a football team who you both support (the players, the manager, recent fixtures, an upcoming match, etc.)

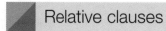

# Relative clauses

E P I U- **Defining**

► Find the connections.

| I want a car | where | I can rely on. |
| I want to live in a town | which | you showed me yesterday. |
| I want a friend | that | the people are friendly. |
| I want the one | who | is safe and economical. |

In pairs, tell each other about things you've got, places you've been to, and people you know, e.g. *I've got a mobile phone that takes photos. I once went to a place where everyone carries a gun. I know someone who can ride a monocycle.*

► In two groups, write ten questions to quiz the other group with. You must use each of these pronouns at least once, e.g. *Name the country where Einstein was born. Name the pers who painted the 'Mona Lisa'.*

> that, which, whose, when, who, where

E P I U- **Definitions**

I'm going to read some definitions. Write down the thing or person I'm defining, e.g. A pla where you can buy food. – *Supermarket.*

| | |
| --- | --- |
| a place where you can eat | something that opens doors |
| a person who opens doors | an animal which has big ears |
| a place where people are buried | a person whose wife has died |
| a day when nobody works | a time when people celebrate |
| a person who arrests people | a place where you can see animals |
| a person who lives in a palace | a place where you keep money |
| a city where they speak French | a person whose job is to teach |

Work in pairs. Try to remember the definitions, e.g. supermarket – *A supermarket is a place where you can buy groceries.*

E P I U- **Bluff words**

In teams of three, find a word in the dictionary that you are sure nobody in class knows and write three definitions, two false and one correct, e.g. bluff.

1) *A bluff is a soft stick that you use for hitting a drum.*
2) *Bluff is a colour which is mid-way between blue and grey.*
3) *To bluff is to make someone believe something that is untrue.*

Take turns to read your definitions. The other teams have to choose one of your definitions If they choose one of your false definitions, your team wins a point. If they choose the correct one, they win a point.

(Variation: Choose words from the list below. Your selection should include things, people and places. Finish the activity by writing up more words and asking for imaginative definitions from the whole class.)

> blacksmith, flea, fluff, harvest, hinge, hive, hook, idler, janitor, kennel, kiln, kipper, kite, larder, lobster, loo, maggot, maze, miser, outcast, ox, padlock, paw, ploughman, potty, pram, ragamuffin, sawmill, sewer, skip, socket, spanner, spinster, swap, teetotaller, thorn, thug, tickle, toddler, trap, twig, undertaker, venue, whip, wig, yawn

E P I U

## Favourite things

▶ In small groups, tell each other about these things, e.g. an animal that you like – *The Siberian Tiger is an animal that I really like because …*

| | |
|---|---|
| a place where you like to relax | someone who you admire |
| a time when you felt really happy | something that you are good at |
| a book which you enjoyed | an animal that you like |
| a place where you would like to be | something which you have found useful |

▶ In three groups, brainstorm ten to fifteen words in the categories I give you, and write them on small pieces of paper.

Group A: household objects
Group B: famous people
Group C: places (countries, cities, monuments, etc.)

(Collect all the pieces of paper together and shuffle them. Divide them into four piles again and put one pile in the middle of each group.) Take turns to pick up a piece of paper and make a sentence,e.g. *Picasso was the person who painted 'Guernica'.* If you make a grammatically and factually correct sentence in fifteen seconds, you get to keep the piece of paper. If you can't make a correct sentence, put the piece of paper back at the bottom of the pile. The person at the end with the most pieces of paper is the winner.

P I U

## Non-defining

▶ In small groups, join these pairs of sentences, e.g. The old boathouse is a museum now. Dylan Thomas lived there. – *The old boathouse, where Dylan Thomas lived, is a museum now.*

Sandra is my best friend. I went to school with her.
We went on holiday to Greece. We spent a week just sunbathing.
The man asked me for a lift. His car had broken down.
We threw out our old TV and bought another. It had stopped working.
A mate got me this car. His brother's a mechanic.

On your own, write similar pairs of sentences which are true for you. Pass them to your partner, e.g. *My dad's a chemist. He works for Lukoil.* Look at the pairs of sentences you receive, and join them to make one, e.g. *My dad, who's a chemist, works for Lukoil.*

▶ In groups of three, write a few questions that you might ask someone about each of these things, e.g. *Do you like collecting things?*

hobbies and collecting things, nightlife and going out, favourite TV programmes and films, food and cooking, holidays and travel, friends and family, favourite books and authors, professions and skills, likes and ambitions, possessions and money

(Put an empty seat in the middle of the class and choose a student to sit there. The rest of the class asks him/her questions based on their group work. When they have gleaned a few facts from the student in the middle, elicit a non-defining relative clause and write it on the board, as in the example below. Then ask the student in the middle to choose another to take his/her place, and keep repeating the process until everyone has had a go.)

Class – *Do you like dancing, Annette?*
Annette – *Yes. I love it.*
Class – *Are you any good?*
Annette – *Not really. But I go to a nightclub every weekend.*
*Annette, who loves dancing, goes to a nightclub every weekend.*

E P I U+ **Elaboration**

► I'm going to dictate a short story. I'll stop after each sentence. Write the sentence and try to add a relative clause, e.g. I met an old friend called Pete. – *I met an old friend called Pete, who(m) I hadn't seen for ten years.*

> On Saturday I visited my old school. I went with my friend Mark. We drove down in his Mini. We stopped on the way in Oxford. When we arrived we met the headmaster and his wife. We had lunch at the pub. It was in the local village. In the evening, we drove to Cheltenham. The next morning we returned to London.

Compare your sentences with a partner.

► Work in pairs. Copy the form and interview your partner in order to complete it. Write four sentences about him/her using relative clauses, e.g. *Yukiko, who qualified as a graphic designer, works for Dreamworks.* When you have finished, swap sentences with your partner to check facts.

> Name _____
>
> Country of birth _____        Countries visited _____
>
> Qualifications _____        Job _____
>
> Marital status _____        Children _____
>
> Languages _____        Level of English _____

E P I U+ **Whatever, whenever**

Write endings for these sentences using *whatever, whenever, whoever, however* or *wherever*. In pairs, take turns to read one of your endings and see if your partner can guess which sentence it's from.

> I will think of you ...          Neil gets up ...          In London people dress ...
> I want to speak to ...          We can meet ...          Jimmy couldn't do it ...
> Help yourself to ...          Rose will marry ...          My dog doesn't obey me ...

Change five of your sentences so that they are true for you.

## Reported speech

E P I U+ **Feedback**

In pairs, ask and answer questions about the following topics. Make some notes. Then pair up with a new partner and tell each other what you learnt about the first partner, e.g.

A – *What kind of music do you like?*
B – *Jazz, mainly.*
A – *I asked Potey what kind of music he liked and he said he liked jazz.*

> likes/dislikes, last night's dinner, plans for tomorrow, yesterday's lesson, next week, what you did last weekend, next year, family, life experiences (Have you ever ...?), the weekends, hobbies, food, your country

## Contradictions

Listen to these statements. Take turns to contradict me, e.g. T – *I'm married.* A – *But you told me you were single!* T – *Oh dear! It's raining.* B – *What?! They said it would be sunny.*

| | |
|---|---|
| He can't speak English. | I'll be back at 10.30. |
| I can't come to your party. | There's no milk left. |
| I'm 25 years old. | That'll be €100, please. |
| My brother's a barman. | I've decided to marry Yvonne. |
| The exam is tomorrow. | I don't know where we are. |
| His ticket says he arrived on the 4th. | The meeting is on the 20th. |

Write five similar sentences. In pairs, take turns to read out your sentences and contradict each other.

## Gossip ⚠

Work in pairs. Tell each other two lies about other students in the class, e.g. *Misha sleeps with a teddy bear.*

Mingle and tell each other the lies you heard about them. If you hear a lie about yourself, confront the liar. If you are accused of lying, deny it, e.g.

Kara – *Misha, Roberto said you slept with your teddy bear.*
Misha – *Hey, Roberto. Why did you tell Kara I slept with a teddy bear?*
Roberto – *I didn't say you slept with a teddy bear now; I said you had slept with a teddy bear when you were a child.*

## News reports

In groups, brainstorm some recent statements by politicians and celebrities, e.g. *The minister promised to get tough on crime. The soap star denied that she was having an affair.*

Here are some reporting verbs to help you.

accuse, deny, claim, insist, promise, agree, admit

## Holiday reps

What kinds of things are included in a package holiday?

accommodation, flights and transfers, meals, excursions, entertainment, child care, travel insurance

In pairs, imagine you have just been on the 'holiday from hell'. Brainstorm a list of things you are unhappy about from your holiday. Write a letter of complaint to the holiday company, dealing with each item, e.g. *We were told we would have a room with a view, but it faced a building site! You said the hotel had a pool. You didn't tell us it would be empty!*

Swap letters with another pair. Who had the worst holiday?

## Go-between ⚠

Imagine you are the go-between in a relationship between two people who have just split up. You are delivering a message from one person to the other saying why he/she wants her/him back. Work in pairs and write your message as a note, e.g. *John's heart is broken. He said he'd been thinking about you all the time and he couldn't sleep because of it. He said he would do anything to have you back … .* Read out your message. As a class, decide whose note is the saddest.

## So

E P I U+ **So and such**

▶ I'm going to read out some sentences with *so*. In pairs, guess what I'm talking about and write a sentence with *such*, e.g. *It's so hot.* – *It's such a hot day.*

| | | |
|---|---|---|
| It was so nice. | They're so beautiful. | She's so nice. |
| That was so easy. | It was so strange. | That's so stupid! |
| It's so strong. | He is so interesting. | This is so difficult. |

▶ In groups of three, take turns to make sentences using these two groups of words and alternating *so* and *such*, e.g. A – *His car is so slow.* B – *He's got such a slow car.* C – *London is so cold.* A – *London is such a cold city.*

| | |
|---|---|
| job, London, day, Camilla, journey, film, house | nice, exiting, big, long, dangerous, boring, dull |

▶ Imagine you are having a drink after work. You are 'talking shop'. Discuss these things using *so* and *such*, e.g. *The boss is so bad tempered.*

> the boss, the workload, the canteen, a client, the secretary, the building/office, the pay, a colleague, the office party

▶ (In open class.) Imagine you are all riding together in a limo on your way home from a fantastic party. Shout out comments using *so* and *such*, e.g. *That was such a great party!*

In two groups, make similar excited comments about these things. (Let group A finish their comments about the first thing before asking group B to comment about theirs. Then ask group B to comment first about the next thing.)

> Group A: an awful meal in a restaurant, a holiday from hell, a brilliant football match, a wonderful teacher
>
> Group B: a great meal in a restaurant, a holiday in paradise, a disastrous football match, a terrible teacher

E P I U+ **So ... that**

▶ In groups of four, brainstorm a list of twelve adjectives. Follow this sequence to build sentences, e.g.

A – *Sad.*
B – *I'm so sad.*
C – *I'm so sad that I could cry.*
D – *Hard.*
A – *It's so hard.*
B – *It's so hard that I think I'll give up.*
C – *Easy ...*

▶ In groups of four, brainstorm a list of twelve nouns. Follow this sequence to build sentences, e.g.

A – *Film.*
B – *It's such a good film.*
C – *It's such a good film that I could watch it again and again.*
D – *Game.*
A – *It was such an exciting game.*

## so/too and neither/either

P | I | U+

### Information exchange

▶ (Write the table on the board with the first two rows of sentences and examples only.) Copy the table. I'm going to dictate some sentences. Write them in the first column. After each one I'll give you a few moments to write the short agreements in the next two columns.

|  | so/neither | too/either |
|---|---|---|
| I study English. | So do I. | I do too. |
| I don't get up early. | Neither do I. | I don't either. |
| I live in a flat. | | |
| He doesn't like sport. | | |
| I'm studying here. | | |
| We went to Leicester. | | |
| I didn't like the film. | | |
| We'll be at the carnival. | | |
| They won't go. | | |
| I've got a degree. | | |
| I haven't got a clue. | | |
| His eyes are brown. | | |

Check your answers with a partner. Take turns to close your notebooks and be tested. Student A, read out the sentences. Student B, reply with *so/neither* and *too/either*.

▶ In groups of three, talk about these topics and find out whether your colleagues agree or disagree. (Model the intonation in the example.)

A – *I like this room.*
B – *So do I. / I do too.*
C – *Oh, I don't.*
B – *I can't swim.*
C – *Neither can I. / I can't either.*
A – *Really? I can.*

> possessions, abilities, likes/dislikes, your country, hobbies, family, plans for tomorrow, your job, experiences, what you did yesterday

P | I | U+

### Things in common

▶ In pairs, find out how much you have in common using these cues, e.g.

A – *I like swimming.*
B – *So do I. I go every day.*

| I like ... | I'm not ... | I can ... | I can't ... |
|---|---|---|---|
| I've got ... | I went ... | I'm going to ... | I'm ... |
| I've been ... | I don't like ... | I'd like ... | I've never ... |

▶ In pairs, imagine you are a couple on a first date. You are asking each other all about your likes and opinions, and you find that they are exactly the same! Role-play the conversation.

## Both and neither

▶ In pairs, discuss the topics below and then report back to the class on the things that you both do and the things neither of you does, e.g.

A – *I play chess.*
B – *So do I. / I do too.*
A – *We both play chess.*

A – *I don't play chess.*
B – *Neither do I. / I don't either.*
A – *Neither of us plays chess.*

> speak Spanish, fail an exam, learn English, know what *fluff* means,
> fly in a helicopter, drive, go to the Galapagos, like bonfires, have a job,
> attend every lesson so far, play cricket, eat meat, wear jeans, smoke

▶ In pairs, discuss the six items in each group and choose two that are different. Say why using *both* or *neither*, e.g. gin, water, wine, brandy, coke, whisky – *Brandy and wine because they are both made in France. Water and coke because neither of them is alcoholic.*

> 1 lemon, potato, banana, orange, onion, strawberry
> 2 ostrich, bee, cow, bat, owl, butterfly
> 3 Rome, Paris, Montreal, Chicago, Naples, Dublin
> 4 violin, cello, flute, saxophone, electric guitar, bass
> 5 stool, table, desk, bench, chair, sofa

Compare your answers with another pair. Work together as a group and write another set of six words. Read them out and see if anyone in class can find the two that don't fit.

(Choose six students in the class and elicit similar sentences, e.g. *Eva and John because they both walk to school.*)

## All/none ... except

On your own, write three questions about everyday habits and routines. Get into groups of four and conduct a mini-survey of the other three. Then write a few sentences about your group, e.g. *We all eat cornflakes except Nuria. None of us has a cooked breakfast except Yukio.*

## There is/are

## Imagine

Work in pairs. Take turns to close your eyes and imagine the perfect house or holiday location. Describe it to your partner, e.g. *There's a beautiful garden with a little cottage in the middle of it. There are some apple trees. There are lots of birds singing everywhere. There's a fountain in the middle ...*

Ask your partner questions about his/her imaginary place, e.g. A – *Are there any animals?* B – *Yes, there are. I can hear lots of birds.* A – *Is there a pond?* B – *No, there isn't, but there's a fountain.*

## Describe and draw

▶ I need a volunteer to draw the things in my home. (Draw a plan of your home on the board and give the volunteer a board pen.) Draw these things, e.g. *There's a table in the kitchen. There are some plants in the living room.* (List about five.)

Work in pairs. Draw a floor plan of your home and give it to your partner. Tell one another where ten things are and see if they can draw them on your plan.

▶ In pairs, ask each other questions about the places you live, e.g. *Is there a table in the kitchen? Are there any plants in the living room?*

## Too much/many and not enough

P | I | U+

### Complaints

► Add a line of explanation to these complaints using *too much/many* or *not enough*, e.g. I don't like this classroom. – *There are too many of us and not enough chairs.*

| | |
|---|---|
| This coffee is terrible. | This is a poor country. |
| You're fired! | I need a bigger flat. |
| I can't come out tonight. | She's got thirteen children. |
| It's no fun working here. | I don't like living on a farm. |

► In pairs, tell each other about things you don't like and why, e.g. *I don't like the weather. There's too much rain and not enough sunshine.*

> this country, your job, life in a big city, a celebrity, the weather, the food, the place where you live

P | I | U+

### A perfect world

In small groups, make a list of ten problems in the world and briefly explain them, e.g. 1) War – *There isn't enough cooperation between governments.* 2) Pollution – *People drive their cars too much.* Do this on the left-hand side of a piece of paper.

Swap lists with another group. Discuss solutions and write them on the right-hand side, e.g. 1) *We need to give more power to the UN.* 2) *More people should ride bicycles.*

Swap lists again to see if you agree with the other group's solutions.

P | I | U+

### Too + adjective ⚠

► Tell me some jobs and two adjectives for each, e.g. Teacher – *patient, organised.* (Write them up until you have about ten jobs.)

In pairs, tell each other why people you know couldn't do those jobs, e.g. *My brother would be a terrible teacher. He's too impatient and not organised enough.*

► On a piece of paper, write down two things about yourself that you'd like to change using *too* + adjective, e.g. *I'm (a bit) too disorganised.* (Collect the pieces of paper.)

I'm going to read them out. In pairs, guess who it is each time.

## Used to

P | I | U+

### Changes

In three groups, list the ways life used to be different, e.g. *1,000 years ago most people used to go everywhere on foot.*

Group A, talk about life 100 years ago.
Group B, talk about life 1,000 years ago.
Group C, talk about life 10,000 years ago.

Here are some ideas to help you.

> transport, politics, food, work, health, education

Pass your list to the next group and see if you can add anything to the list that is passed to your group.

**Life-changing events** ⚠

► In pairs, brainstorm five life-changing events, eg. winning the lottery. Shout out your ideas. (Write the best ones on the board.) Each pair, choose an important event from the list. Each pair must choose a different event. Write five sentences about how life used to be different, with a corresponding sentence about how things are nowadays, e.g. *I used to count my pennies. Now I can't count how much money I've got.*

Read out your list of sentences, but do not mention the life-changing event. Other students will guess what it was.

► Write about ten sentences describing how your relationships have changed in the last ten years, e.g. *I used to go out with someone called Simon. Now I'm married to Paul. I didn't use to be as close to my brother as I am now.*

In small groups, tell each other about the changes you wrote down. Are there any trends in common? (If possible, group students of a similar age together.)

**News**

I'm going to tell you some surprising news about people you haven't seen for a long time. Take turns to say why you're surprised, e.g. T – *Christine has taken up acting.* S – *Really? She used to be so shy.*

| | |
|---|---|
| Michael's got a dog now. | Sue is studying to be a doctor. |
| Terry's looking much healthier. | Janet's pregnant. |
| Adrian has bought a big house. | Penny plays the bass guitar now. |
| Lisa's going out with Tom. | I saw Allan. He's got married, you know. |
| Veronica has become an actress. | William's joined the Conservative party. |
| We're divorced now, I'm afraid. | You know Ray, don't you? That's him there. |
| I saw Angela at Rachel's place. | Roger has taken up sailing. |
| Ellen's become a Buddhist. | This isn't my natural hair colour, you know. |
| I'm reading Shakespeare's plays. | Daniel is studying law these days. |

**Question focus**

In small groups, ask each other questions about how you've changed in the last five years, e.g.

A – *Did you used to have a much different hairstyle five years ago?*
B – *Oh, yes. I used to dye my hair all the time, too. Once I even dyed it green!*

> physical appearance (clothes, hair, build)
> habits (food, smoking, alcohol, going out)
> personality (problems, hopes, fears)
> people (friends, family, heroes and heroines)

**Childhood**

► In pairs, tell each other about when you were young children, e.g. *When I was young I used to get pocket money every Saturday. I didn't used to like eating vegetables.*

> naughty, housework, tooth fairy, best friend, favourite toys, thumb sucking,
> fighting with a brother/sister, imaginary friends, being afraid of the dark,
> parents, Father Christmas, favourite games, bedtime, favourite food

► Who used to believe strange things when they were little? Tell us about them, e.g. *I used to think that cats and dogs got married.*

**Schooldays**

In pairs, ask each other questions about your schooldays, e.g. *Did you use to play truant often?*
Here are some expressions to help you.

> love school, love sports, study hard, be a bully, have a strict teacher,
> be good at music, make trouble, smoke cigarettes, wear a tie, be lazy,
> do lines or detention, have a funny teacher, be the teacher's pet

**Antiques fair**

Work in groups of three. Imagine you are antiques experts in the year 3000. I'm going to
tell you some objects. (Where possible, use realia.) Try to invent reasonable but false
descriptions of what people used to do with them, e.g. rubber band – *In the mid-nineteenth
century, people used to chew these to clean their teeth after eating.*

> a CD, a training shoe, a cigarette, a yo-yo, a pair of glasses,
> a credit card, a toothpick, a mobile phone, a bunch of keys,
> a coin, a comb, a fork, a die, a teddy bear, a floppy disk

# Vocabulary

## Adjectives

### Nice people, nasty people

Look at this conversation.

> A – I like my cousin Roger.
> B – Why?
> A – Because he always sends cards and gives me lots of presents.
> B – So you like him because he's generous.
> A – That's right.

Work in pairs. Take turns to describe someone you know and see if your partner can think of the right adjective. Here are some adjectives to help you.

> honest, modest, careless, moody, positive, selfish, insecure, easy-going, rude, cheerful, creative, hard-working, kind, boring, aggressive, polite

### Someone who ... ⚠

Listen to this list of twenty descriptions of people. For each one, shout out an adjective that describes the person, then write down the number and name of someone you know who is like that. Don't write the adjective.

> Someone who ...
> 1  keeps losing things (careless, forgetful, absent-minded)
> 2  always drops/breaks things (clumsy)
> 3  thinks bad things will happen (pessimistic, negative)
> 4  goes to a lot of parties (outgoing, sociable, gregarious)
> 5  keeps to himself (introverted, unsociable, withdrawn, closed)
> 6  never smiles (moody, grumpy, bad-tempered, miserable)
> 7  makes you yawn (boring, uninteresting, dull)
> 8  likes making things (creative, artistic)
> 9  keeps things tidy (neat, organised, efficient)
> 10  never thinks about others' feelings (uncaring, insensitive, selfish)
> 11  always arrives late for meetings, etc. (unpunctual, unreliable)
> 12  makes you laugh all the time (funny, humorous, silly)
> 13  thinks good things will happen (optimistic, positive)
> 14  hurts people or animals (cruel, sadistic, mean)
> 15  doesn't like talking about her achievements (modest, unassuming)
> 16  is easy to get on with (friendly, affable, easygoing)
> 17  brags about himself a lot (conceited, arrogant, big-headed)
> 18  never changes her mind even when she knows she's wrong (stubborn, obstinate)
> 19  never gives presents or buys drinks (mean, tight-fisted)
> 20  always cries at weddings, in the cinema, etc. (emotional, sentimental, hysterical)

For each person in your list, write the adjective from memory. Then compare your ideas with a partner. Tell each other about the people on your list, with examples of their typical behaviour.

In your pairs, think of a famous person for each adjective.

P I U+ **Verbs and adjectives**

In small groups, tell each other things that …

> scare you, annoy you, offend you, depress you, amuse you, shock you, bore you, relax you, impress you, embarrass you, surprise you, confuse you, interest you

e.g. *I'm scared of mice.*

Think of a time when you felt one of these emotions and tell the group about it.

P I U+ **People and places**

► Work in two groups, A and B. I'm going to say some nouns. Group A, shout out a positive adjective for each one. Group B shout out a negative one, e.g. rock star. A – *famous.* B – *rude.*

> house, baby, tramp, shirt, river, dog, tree, hair, pig, car, shoe, girl, flower, park, street, town, litter

► In pairs, think of a place you both know. Student A, write a positive description of the place. Student B, write a negative one. Compare your descriptions.

## Animals

P I U+ **Animal characteristics**

► In pairs, match each animal with the adjective which is traditionally used to describe them. (Re-order the adjectives when you write them up on the board; they appear here in the correct order.)

> owl, fox, mouse, monkey, lion, dog, bat, ox, donkey, dinosaur, pig, cat, fish

> wise, clever, small, cheeky, proud, loyal, blind, strong, stubborn, extinct, greedy, independent, slippery

How do they compare with popular ideas about animals in your country, e.g. *Is an owl considered wise?*

► Think of animals that these adjectives could describe.

> lazy, thoughtful, selfish, kind, sensible, sensitive, posh, cold, cheerful, impatient, hard-working, easy-going, stylish, reserved, antisocial, moody

Think of another adjective to describe each animal and explain why you chose it.

P I U+ **Animal categories**

Work in teams. I'm going to give you a category of animals, e.g. animals that can fly. Agree how many different animals in that category your team can write down in two minutes. The team which bids the highest number goes first. If they reach that number, they win that many points. If they don't, they don't get any points and the other teams get one point for each different animal on their lists.

> Animals that: lay eggs, are very strong, dig holes, are poisonous, live in people's houses, people eat, eat people, are noisy, hibernate

**Definitions**

▶ Choose five of these animals and write two sentences about each, one with *are* and one with *can*. Don't write the name of the animal, e.g. *They are covered in feathers. Most of them can fly* (birds).

> bees, hippopotamuses, horses, whales, snakes, spiders, owls, bats, ostriches, monkeys, cats, dogs, butterflies

In small groups, read your sentences to the others and see if they can guess the animal.

▶ Work in pairs. Imagine you are an animal, but don't tell your partner which one. Continue these sentences and see if you partner can guess what you are.

> I live in ...                    At night I ...
> I'm afraid of ...              I can ...
> During the day I ...         I eat ...
> I normally live for ...      ... are afraid of me.

▶ Work in small groups. Agree definitions of these groups of animals, and write them down.

> mammals, birds, insects, fish, reptiles

Pass your definitions to another group. See if you can find exceptions to the definitions you are given.

**Animal language**

What does this mean? – *Cock-a-doodle-doo!* Clues: It's an animal call, and it happens in the morning. What does a cockerel say in your language?

In pairs, look at these words and imagine which animals say them.

> woof, moo, oink, miaow, baaa, tweet

What are the sounds in your language? What about some other animals?

**Animal kingdom**

Work on your own. Copy this diagram. Write your favourite and your least favourite animal for each of these categories: flying, walking and swimming. Compare your choices with your partner and tell each other why you chose them.

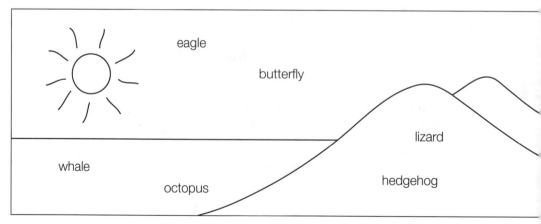

eagle

butterfly

lizard

whale

octopus

hedgehog

### Ten things

► Work in two teams and choose someone to come to the board to write. I'll read out some categories. In your team, quickly think of ten things in that category. Then the person comes to the board and writes the list. The first team to write the list wins a point.

> Things that: come in pairs, can fly, float in water, move fast, you keep cold, are symmetrical, make a lot of noise

► In two teams, take turns to shout out words in these categories. The last team to think of one wins a point. (Set a time limit for the last item.)

> Things that: are invisible, you can't buy, are soft, can be full or empty, have holes, are difficult, fit together, make you feel good, go up and down

### Odds and ends

Work in small groups. I'll give each group a place. Write a list of ten items that you can find there.

> a woman's hangbag, an office desk drawer, a hiker's backpack, a child's pocket

Take turns to name the place and give the other groups one minute to shout out everything they think is on your list. Your group gets one point for everything on your list that the others don't think of.

Brainstorm some objects which can be found in more than one of the places. Bearing this in mind, agree on the single most useful thing in the world, e.g. a piece of string.

### Going, going ... gone

► Work in teams. I'm going to give you the first word in a category. Take turns to shout out more words in the same category, e.g. uncle – *son, sister* ... . The last team to give a word wins a point. (When someone starts to stall, finish the category by saying *Going, going ... gone.* This is the last thing an auctioneer says to stop bidding.)

> arm, tennis, doctor, hat, who, table, you, rain, happy, across, red, apple, bedroom

► (Write five categories on the board, e.g. things you find in the kitchen, things you take to the beach, etc. Ask students to write the categories as column headings. Say random words belonging to these categories and students write them in the correct columns. Ask individual students to give other words for the rest of the class to add to their lists.)

### A to Z

Work in groups of six or seven. Choose one of these categories and take turns to name a member of the category starting with the letter *a* and working through the alphabet, e.g. animals – *ant, butterfly, cat.* If you can't think of one, you are out of the game. The last three left get a point. Then choose another category and repeat.

> animals, food, nationalities, adjectives, rooms and furniture, clothes, verbs

(Variation: The word has to begin with the last letter of the previous word, e.g. *giraffe, elephant, tiger.*)

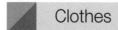

## Clothes

E P I U· **Kinds of clothes**

What does the rhyme 'Something old, something new, something borrowed, something blue' refer to? (Answer: Traditional advice to a bride on what to wear at her wedding.)

In small groups, think of the best clothes for these situations.

> a walk in the snow, a cocktail party, a job interview, a naming ceremony (including the baby's clothes), a camel ride in the desert, a night at the disco, an expedition into the jungl

Tell each other about a time you had to dress up for a formal occasion or a special event.

E P I U· **My clothes**

► Find someone in class who is wearing …

> something green, designer clothes, jeans, nylon, sandals, no socks, silk, a belt, something striped

I will tell each of you the name of someone else in class. On your own, write a description of what this person is wearing. (Collect the descriptions and read them out to see how quickly the class can identify each person.)

► Point to these things, either on yourself or on another student.

> zip, pocket, button, collar, laces, sleeve, hem, heel, lapel

Find out who has got:

> the most zips, the deepest pockets, the brightest socks, the longest laces, the highest heels, the biggest lapels/collar, the most interesting buttons

► Everybody stand up. Sit down if you are wearing the things I say. The last person standing is the winner. (Read out the list one at a time. Vary or add to the list according to what your students are wearing.)

> green socks, a jacket with zips, a belt, trainers, jeans, a blue shirt, a sweatshirt with a logo, high heels, a short-sleeved top, something with more than six buttons, a baseball cap

E P I U· **Describing clothes**

Listen to the following words and put them in five categories: opinion, age, colour, pattern or style, and material.

> denim, flared, baggy, scruffy, leather, lovely, new, blue, nice, nylon, pink, plain, plastic, purple, silk, casual, second-hand, short-sleeved, polka-dot, striped, old-fashioned, smart, trendy, velvet, wool, cotton, awful, checked

In pairs, compare your lists and add more words to each category.

Describe to each other what some of the other students are wearing using several of the adjectives in your list, e.g. *She's wearing a beautiful, green, silk skirt. He's got new baggy jeans.*

Who is the best-dressed person in the class?

Tell us about a traditional costume from your country.

**Suits you**

► What does the rhyme 'Red and green should never be seen; not even in a washing machine' refer to? (Answer: Colours which supposedly clash.)

In small groups, talk about which clothes and colours go together and which don't. Tell each other which clothes and colours suit you, and why.

► Discuss the differences between these pairs of words and phrases.

| | | |
|---|---|---|
| inside out / back to front | fashion / style | blouse / shirt |
| hat / cap | to go with / to suit | size / fit |

► In pairs, find out if there's something that one of you wants to buy. Write a short conversation between a customer and a shop assistant in a shop that sells what you want. (Invite several pairs to read out their conversation.)

**Specialist outfitters**

► In pairs, think of an occasion which requires special clothes, e.g. a wedding, a walk in the mountains. Discuss what clothing advice you would give someone who was coming with you. Join a pair planning a different outing. Take turns to give each other advice on what to wear for the two trips.

Whose trip needed the most specialist or expensive clothes? In your groups, tell each other about any specialist clothing you have.

► Write an appropriate activity for each of these items. Compare your ideas with a partner.

> goggles, mittens, shin guards, flippers, helmet, bow tie, sweatband,
> apron, lifejacket, veil, wetsuit, nappies, wellington boots,
> high-heeled shoes, tracksuit, sandals, dressing gown, trainers

Tell each other about a time when you wore some of these things. Make a note of what your partner has worn and at the end we'll see who in the class has worn the most items.

## Colours

**Classroom colours**

► In pairs, write a list of things in the classroom which are …

> yellow, dark green, red, light blue, orange, dark blue, brown,
> black, pink, grey, white, mauve, light green, purple

► In teams, write a list of things that are the colour I say, e.g. *white – snow, paper, golf balls*, etc. I'll give you thirty seconds before I say another colour. Your team will get a point for each thing that the other teams didn't put. The team with the most points is the winner.

**I'm blue**

► In pairs, discuss what these expressions with the colour blue mean. Check them in a dictionary, if necessary. Then discuss a situation in which you could use each one.

> to look blue, to do something till you are blue in the face, once in a blue moon,
> out of the blue, to be black and blue, the boys in blue, to scream blue murder

Look up other expressions with different colours in your dictionary, e.g. *to be blacklisted, to be green with envy, a grey area, to see red, a white lie, a yellow streak*. Think of a time when one of these expressions would have been appropriate for you. Tell your partner.

**United colours**

In small groups, answer these questions and explain your answers.

> 1 Which colours don't go together?
> 2 What colours are there in your room/flat/house?
> 3 What colours make people feel sad/happy/aggressive?
> 4 What colour socks are you wearing today? Don't look!
> 5 What colours are there in your national flag? What do they symbolise?
> 6 What do different colours signify in your culture?
> 7 What colour are these words: love, death, happiness, hunger, wealth, sleep?
> 8 What's your favourite colour? Why?

**Mixed colours**

In small groups, agree the answers to these questions and note them down. Some questions have more than one answer. Score one point per colour.

> 1 What do you get if you mix blue and yellow? (green)
> 2 What colour is the planet Mars? (red)
> 3 What do you get if you mix red and green? (brown)
> 4 What do you get if you mix black and white? (grey)
> 5 What colour are my eyes? (Close them and see who can remember.)
> 6 What kind of colour is scarlet? (red)
> 7 What colour are New York taxis? (yellow)
> 8 What are the colours of the rainbow? (red, orange, yellow, green, blue, indigo, violet)
> 9 What kind of colour is turquoise? (blue)
> 10 What colour are baby girls traditionally dressed in? (pink, yellow, white)
> 11 What do you get if you mix red and yellow? (orange)
> 12 What colour is the Financial Times? (pink)
> 13 What colour are tulips? (red, yellow, orange, white, 'black')
> 14 What do you get if you mix blue and red? (purple)

## Computers

**Word processing**

► In small groups, find examples of the following in your course book.

> bold, font, paragraph, italic, line, capital letter, underline, strikethrough, superscript

► (If you have access to a computer in class, open up a blank Word document.) In small groups, show each other where to find these options.

> tab, copy, paste, cut, return, delete, edit, cursor, zoom, open, save, select, print

**My computer**

(Draw a computer and its accessories on the board and ask students to name each thing.)

> screen/monitor, computer, keyboard, mouse, mouse mat, printer, scanner, CD drive, floppy disk drive, modem port

◻ I U· **The Internet**

▶ In small groups, imagine you are going to give a course on how to use the Internet to a class of complete beginners. Before you start, you want to explain the following vocabulary. Prepare your notes.

> ISP (Internet Service Provider), password, to log on, virus, hacker, links, spam, to browse, to download, online, website, surf, bandwidth, worldwide web, home page, HTTP (Hypertext Transfer Protocol)

Compare your notes with another group. Who has the clearest explanations?

▶ In small groups, write a list of the top ten uses of the Internet. Compare your lists.

◻ I U· **Punctuation**

Work in pairs. Match the symbols on the left with their names on the right. (Re-order the words in the second box when you write them up; they appear here in the correct order.)

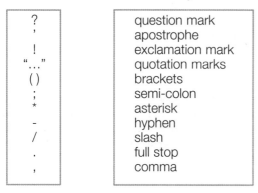

| ? | question mark |
|---|---|
| , | apostrophe |
| ! | exclamation mark |
| " ... " | quotation marks |
| ( ) | brackets |
| ; | semi-colon |
| * | asterisk |
| - | hyphen |
| / | slash |
| . | full stop |
| , | comma |

Using a passage of English writing, find examples of punctuation and explain how they demonstrate the rules.

## Definitions

◻ I U· **Love is ...**

Work in small groups. Write suitable endings for these definitions.

| | | | |
|---|---|---|---|
| Love is ... | A friend is ... | Time is ... | Art is ... |
| Life is ... | Dogs are ... | Music is ... | Children are ... |
| Religion is ... | Being old is ... | Happiness is ... | Being young ... |

Read out just your endings and see if the class can guess what they define.

◻ I U· **Confusing words**

In pairs, write sentences to demonstrate the differences between these pairs of words, e.g. *He's robbed about 20 people. In total, he's stolen about €500.*

> rob/steal, rise/raise, error/fault, bring/take, lie/lay, say/tell, passed/past, sensible/sensitive, principle/principal, presently/actually, luck/chance, wear/put on, watch/see, loose/lose

Are any of these 'false friends' in your language? Tell us any other false friends you've got. (This will be most relevant to students who speak Latin based/influenced languages.)

**Lend and borrow**

Go around the class and try to get the following things from other students, using *borrow/lend*. Explain why you need them, e.g. *Can I borrow your pen? I can't find mine.*

> a pen, a car, glasses, a baby, a sock, a bag, a bicycle,
> notes, a passport, a € 10 note, a dictionary, a calculator

Report back to the class, e.g. *Thierry lent me his sock. I borrowed Maria's watch.*

## Employment

**Work history**

Work in groups. Find out who has had:

> the most jobs, the most complicated job, the most interesting job,
> the most boring job, the most stressful job, a job for the longest

**Town and country**

Work in two groups. Group A, brainstorm city jobs. Group B, brainstorm country jobs. Make sure you both have a copy of the list. Find a partner from the other group and compare lists. If there are any jobs on both lists, explain why you think they should stay on yours instead of your partner's, e.g. *A policeman is needed more in a city than the country.*

**Job application**

In small groups, brainstorm words for a job application. (Build up a word web on the board with words connected to before, during and after the interview.) Then tell each other about a job application you have made.

> CV, job adverts, application form, interview, interview panel,
> pay, contract, probationary period, line manager, promotion

**Job clap**

Stand in a circle. Take turns to name a job, then the workplace for that job, and then another job, and so on, e.g. A – *pilot*. B – *plane*. C – *baker*. Clap your hands to this rhythm (demonstrate) and give your answer on every fourth beat. If you miss the beat, you are out

**Picture board**

Work in two teams. Take turns to come to the board. I'm going to give you a job. (Write it on a piece of paper or whisper it). You have sixty seconds to draw pictures to help your team guess the job. You mustn't write any letters, or speak.

> waiter, doctor, gardener, bricklayer, policeman, carpenter, soldier,
> artist, receptionist, chef, surgeon, farmer, vet, miner, nurse, secretary

**What's my line?**

Take turns to come to the front and sit facing the class with your back to the board. I'm going to write your job on the board. Ask the class yes/no questions to find out what it is, e.g. *Do I work in an office? Do I make things? Do I wear a uniform?*

## Do-it-yourself

▶ Work in small groups. Imagine you are renovating an old house. Brainstorm jobs that will need doing, e.g. fixing the windows, replacing old kitchen units.

(Find out if anyone has worked in a building job or knows about DIY and invite them to answer questions from the class.)

Work in groups. Imagine you are going to have a house built. Decide which kinds of professionals you will need to do the work. Order them in a list beginning with the architect and finishing with the decorators. Next to each one, write one or two jobs they will do.

## Work places

Work in small groups. I'm going to come round and give each group a work place. Brainstorm a list of words you associate with that place, e.g. school – *staffroom, classroom, students, teacher, playground.* Read out your list for the other groups to guess the workplace.

## Exclamations

### Interjections

(Write these interjections on the board.) How do you say these words? When would you say them?

> Shhh! Ouch! Grrr! Hmm. Oi! Mmm! Tut-tut! Yuk! Phew! Wow! Boo! Oh!

How do you express the same feelings in your language?

Do any of the exclamations above mean something different in your language?

In pairs, write short dialogues finishing with an exclamation, e.g. A – *Hey Gary! Have you caught anything yet?* B – *Shhh!*

### Sound box

(Draw the box, without the example words, on the board. Invite a student to add the words according to where the class thinks they should go.)

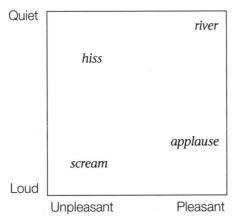

In groups, copy the box and brainstorm more words for it. Try to get an even distribution of words. They can be sounds, e.g. *hiss,* or the things that make sounds, e.g. *snake.*

Leave your sound box on the table and look at what the other groups have done. Make a note of any good words you see on theirs.

**Onomatopoeia**

In pairs, listen to these descriptions. Discuss how you write the sounds in your language and in English, e.g. the sound two cars make as they collide – *Crash!*

> the noise a car horn makes (beep)
> what a cat does when it's happy (purr)
> the noise of a saucepan falling on the floor (clang)
> the sound of frying meat (sizzle)
> what a snake does (hiss)
> the sound you hear when you stick a pin into a balloon (pop)

In pairs, look at these words and say them. Guess what makes each sound. Compare you ideas with another pair.

> buzz, tinkle, squeak, growl, hum, squelch, rustle, crunch, thud

What are some of the 'sound words' in your language?

## Family

**My relatives**

In small groups, tell each other the names of your relatives, e.g. *My dad's name is Alfred.*

> niece, father, sister, brother, aunt, mother, nephew,
> uncle, son, grandfather, daughter, grandmother, cousin

Tell each other what you think your relatives are doing at this moment, e.g. *My brother Da is sitting at his office desk. My aunt Mary is doing the gardening.*

**Family trees**

► In pairs, fill in the names in the royal (Windsor) family tree. (Write up the diagram with all the names blank except Queen Elizabeth.) Compare your work with another group.

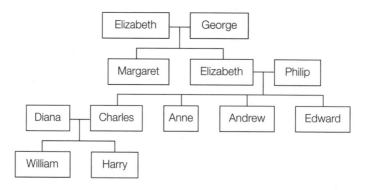

Ask and answer questions about the relationships, e.g. A – *Who's William's aunt?*
B – *William's aunt is Anne.*

► Work in pairs. Describe your family, starting with your grandparents. Your partner will draw your family tree. Then give the family tree to your partner to check.

**Family ties**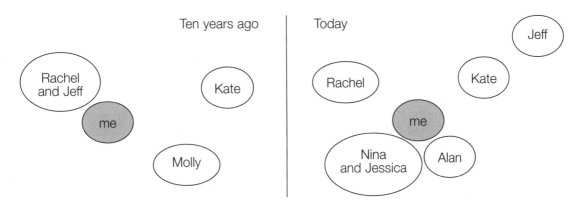

► In groups, discuss the differences between these kinds of family: nuclear family; extended family; single parent family.

What kind of family do you come from? Tell the group about life in your family.

► Draw a diagram like this, showing your family relationships ten years ago and today. The distance between the circles shows the closeness of the relationship. Write the names of the people in your diagram and see if your partner can guess the relationships.

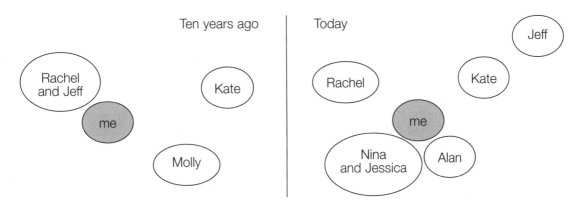

P I U- **Marriage**

Work in small groups. Brainstorm words for this timeline.

Tell each other about a wedding you have been to.

## Food

P I U- **Odd one out**

Work in small groups. I'm going to dictate ten sets of four words, e.g. *cabbage, orange, potato, onion*. After each set, choose the odd one out and circle it. (Give the students a short time to choose between each set. More than one answer is possible.) Take turns to explain your decisions, e.g. *A cabbage, because it's the only one that's green.* / *An orange, because it makes terrible soup.*

| | |
|---|---|
| 1 lemon, grapefruit, grape, lime | 6 scramble, boil, fry, roast |
| 2 fridge, cooker, microwave, toaster | 7 box, bottle, tin, jar |
| 3 Indian, Chinese, French, Italian | 8 cows, chicken, sheep, fish |
| 4 bacon, eggs, tomatoes, toast | 9 rice, wheat, potatoes, pasta |
| 5 bread, cake, pie, pudding | 10 slice, chop, mince, mash |

In your groups, write five more sets and read them out. See if the rest of the class can decide which is the odd one out.

**Food links**

► Match the words and expressions in the two columns. (Re-order the words in the second box when you write them up; they appear here in the correct order.)

| | |
|---|---|
| onions | make you cry |
| bacon | and eggs |
| a dozen | eggs |
| a loaf of | bread |
| salt | and pepper |
| fish | and chips |
| omelette is | made with eggs |
| curry | is spicy |
| caviar | is expensive |
| orange | juice |

► Work in pairs. Copy this list of containers. (Write just the containers on the board.) I'm going to read a list of products; write them next to the correct container.

| | |
|---|---|
| a packet of (biscuits) | a box of (chocolates) |
| a carton of (juice) | a jar of (olives) |
| a tube of (tomato puree) | a bowl of (fruit) |
| a pint of (milk) | a bag of (potatoes) |
| a tin of (sardines) | a bottle of (wine) |

► On your own, complete these expressions, e.g. A piece of – *chocolate*.

a piece of, a bunch of, a loaf of, a slice of, a spoonful of, a cup of, another helping of, a sip of, a bowl of, a handful of, a pinch of

Work with a partner. Take turns to read your words and see if your partner can work out the expression, e.g. A – *Chocolate*. B – *A piece of chocolate*.

**Cooking race**

In small groups, write a ten-item shopping list on a piece of paper. It must include the following things.

something salty, something sweet, a tin of something, a jar of something, a kind of meat or fish, a green vegetable, another vegetable, a fruit, a dairy product, two herbs

Swap lists with another group. You now have ten minutes to agree a recipe for a two-course meal using all the ingredients on their list. You can add only salt, pepper and oil.

Describe your meal to the class. Vote on which meal you would most like to eat.

**Edible or inedible**

In pairs, sit facing each other. Take turns to throw a ball of paper to your partner as you say a noun. When you catch the ball, say immediately if the noun is edible or inedible you must, e.g.

A (throwing) – *Egg*.
B (catching) – *Edible*. (throwing) – *Book*.
A (catching) – *Inedible*. (throwing) *House* …

## Food graph

Work in pairs. Name a kind of food that is …

> cold, sweet, alive, blue, sour, fresh, green, hard, soft, hot, boring, yellow, round, heavy, healthy, unpleasant, expensive, preserved, fattening, junk

Plot the words you came up with on this scattergram.

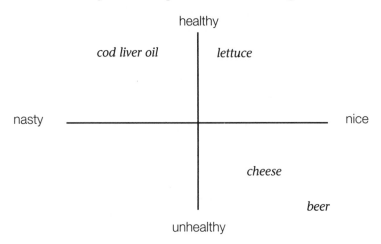

## Geography

### Imaginary features

Look up any of these words you do not know.

> mountain, hill, river, waterfall, valley, cliff, shore, sea, waves, forest, plain, lake, track, quarry, desert, glacier, volcano, island, beach, road

Sit facing each other in pairs. Student A, describe a scene to student B. This can either be a place you have been to, or an imaginary place. Student B, close your eyes and imagine the scene. You need to remember as much detail as possible, so ask questions, e.g. *Is there any snow on the mountains?* When you have finished, swap roles.

(Ask some students to describe their partner's scenes.)

### Outstanding features

Work in small groups. Discuss the answers to these questions and write them down.

> What's the world's …
> highest mountain? (Everest, 8,850 m)    highest waterfall? (Angel Falls, Venezuela, 979 m)
> longest river? (Nile 6,741 km)    driest place? (Calama, Chile. No rain for 400 years)
> biggest city? (Mexico City, 25 million)    deepest place? (Mariana Trench, 11,022 m)
> coldest place? (Antarctica –87.8°C)    biggest island? (Greenland, 2,175,600 km$^2$)
> hottest place? (Al Aziziyah, Lybia, 58°C)    biggest lake? (Caspian Sea, 371,000 km$^2$)

(Go through the answers, giving just the names. Then write up the statistics in a different order and ask the students to match them.)

Tell me the highest mountain, etc. in your country.

## Knowledge race

Work in groups of four and appoint one person to be the secretary. I'm going to name a country. You have one minute to write as many notes as you can about the people and th geography before I name the next country, e.g. China – *big, over a billion people, Great Wall, capital city Beijing.*

> America, Sweden, India, Iceland, Spain, Russia, Brazil, Australia

You have five minutes to turn your notes into complete sentences, e.g. China – *It's a big country. There are over a billion people. The Great Wall is visible from space. The capital city is Beijing.* (Go round and help during this stage.)

Read out your sentences. You score one point for every sentence. You can challenge the other group's sentences on factual accuracy and claim their point.

## Languages

Listen to the countries and write the nationality and the language of each one.
In small groups, compare your lists and write down any words that are new to you.

> Germany (German – German)
> Peru (Peruvian – Spanish, Quechua)
> France (French – French)
> Iran (Iranian – Farsi, Azerbaijani)
> Holland (Dutch – Dutch)
> Japan (Japanese – Japanese)
> Brazil (Brazilian – Portuguese)
> Turkey (Turkish – Turkish, Kurdish)
> Switzerland (Swiss – German, French, Italian, Romance)
>
> Senegal (Senegalese – French, Pulaar, Wolof)
> Wales (Welsh – English, Welsh)
> Canada (Canadian – English, French, Indian)
> Kenya (Kenyan – English, Gikuyu, Swahili ...)
> Israel (Israeli – Hebrew, Arabic)
> Sweden (Swedish – Swedish)
> Ethiopia (Ethiopian – Amharic, Tigrigna)
> Ireland (Irish – English, Gaelic)

## Olympic torch

You are going to describe the journey of the Olympic torch through as many countries as possible. It travels from the city where the Games last took place to the new venue. Take turns to describe the next stage, e.g.

A – *A Greek athlete carried the torch to Istanbul.*
B – *A Turkish athlete carried it to Tehran.*
C – *An Iranian athlete carried it to ...*

## Loan words

Work in small groups. Match the words with the languages they come from. (Re-order the languages when you write them up; they appear here in the correct order.)

> anorak, bamboo, boss, canoe, coach, lilac, mattress, mosquito, sauna, yacht, yoghurt, robot, tomato, pyjamas, kangaroo, whisky, bizarre, piano, zebra, silk, vodka, tycoon
>
> Eskimo, Malay, Dutch, Carib, Hungarian, Farsi, Arabic, Spanish, Finnish, Dutch, Turkish, Czech, Nahuatl, Hindi, Aborigine, Gaelic, Basque, Italian, Swahili, Chinese, Russian, Japanese

Discuss how the words came into the English language. Think about technology, trade, climate and imperialism.

(If the class is mixed nationality, ask them to write a list of English loan words in their languages, and to compare them in groups.)

### Equipment

Work in two groups and brainstorm a list of things you will find in these places. Group A: a first aid kit. Group B: an operating theatre. Make sure everybody in the group writes a copy of the list. (In large classes, you can subdivide the two groups.)

Find a partner from the other group, swap lists and write a use next to each item, e.g. bandage – *It's used to protect a wound.*

Tell each other about any injuries you have had and what was done to remedy them.

### Remedies

▶ Think of five illnesses, and make a list of the symptoms, e.g. cold – *temperature, runny nose, aching joints.*

> measles, hangover, cold, flu, chicken pox, sunstroke, tummy bug, bronchitis

Work in pairs. Take turns to tell your partner your symptoms. Don't say the name of the illness. See if your partner can diagnose the illness and advise you what to do. Decide whether you trust your new doctor.

▶ In pairs, discuss how you would describe these words, e.g. *A thermometer is used to measure temperature. It is often placed in the mouth.*

> injection, aspirin, scalpel, anaesthetic, thermometer, stethoscope, plaster, bandage, sling, x-ray, ice pack

Join another pair and tell each other about any experiences you have had of them.

### Specialists

Think of some words for specialist doctors in your language, e.g. psychiatrist. Guess what the words and spellings are in English. Look up how to spell and pronounce the words and make sure that the jobs are the same as you thought.

In pairs, tell each other some specialisations and see if your partner can tell you what each person deals with.

### Healthy or unhealthy ⚠

▶ Add expressions to this table to show the things you eat and the lifestyle you have.

| Things that are good for you | | Things that are bad for you | |
|---|---|---|---|
| Food | Activities | Food | Activities |
| apples | jogging | too much sugar | overworking |

In pairs, show each other your tables and discuss what changes you would like to make to your lifestyles.

▶ In groups, throw a ball (or a piece of paper) to another student while saying a kind of food or activity. As you catch it, say if the food or activity is healthy or unhealthy, e.g.

A (throwing) – *Crisps.*
B (catching) – *Unhealthy.* (throwing) *Swimming.*
C (catching) – *Healthy.* (throwing) *Playing tennis ...*

**In sickness and in health**

Look at this sequence of events and tell me what happened.

> lose job – unemployed – apply for job – interview – contract –
> office – pay cheque – pay off debts – book holiday

In pairs, write a sequence of words to describe someone's journey from falling seriously ill through to eventual recovery. Use a dictionary, or ask me for words you don't know, and turn your sequence into a narrative about an imaginary friend or relative. Swap partners and read your stories to each other.

If you have been in a similar situation or know someone who has, write about it for homework.

## Holidays

**Things to do**

▶ In groups, brainstorm different kinds of activity holiday, e.g. skiing. (Write each holiday on the board as it is mentioned.) Take turns to tell the class which kinds of holiday you have been on, and answer a few questions about each one.

Copy the holidays down in the order you would like to experience them, from most to least favourite. Compare your list with a partner.

▶ Work in pairs. Imagine you are going on holiday to India, where you will take part in a number of activities. (Elicit activities like these and write them on the board.)

> mountain walking, sightseeing, sunbathing, watching cricket, canoeing,
> nightlife, elephant riding in the jungle, guided tour of Bollywood, yoga

Write two lists: things you need to do before you go, and things you need to take with you. Swap lists with another pair and see how many things they missed.

**Tourist trail**

I'm going to name a country. Take turns around the class to name a tourist attraction there, and then a new country for the next student, e.g.

T – *France.*
A – *The Eiffel tower. India.*
B – *The Taj Mahal. America.*
C – *The Grand Canyon. Brazil …*

In small groups, discuss which of them you have seen or would like to see. Add some more things you like to look at when you travel, e.g. *paintings, street performers.*

On your own, write 100–250 words (choose according to the level of the class) about a time you visited a tourist attraction.

**Flying words**

In small groups, brainstorm words and phrases under these three headings: 1) Before take off, e.g. *check in.* 2) During the flight, e.g. *in-flight entertainment.* 3) After landing, e.g. *baggage reclaim.*

Using as many of the words as you can, tell each other about your last flight, and ask each other questions, e.g. A – *Didn't you watch the film?* B – *No. I'm always asleep when the film is shown.*

**Suitcase game**

(Ask two students to leave the classroom while you give the instructions to the others.)

You are going to name some things to take on holiday, but you can only name things that begin with the same letter as your first name, e.g. **C**arlos can pack a **c**ake, **R**ika can pack a **r**aincoat, etc.

(Ask the two students to come back in. Don't explain the rules to them.)

Take turns to name some things to take on holiday. (Ask each student in turn, including the ones who left the room, what they want to take, asking them each by name. If the students who left don't choose something that begins with the first letter of their name, tell them they can't take that item, but don't tell them why. After a few rounds, if they haven't worked out the rule, make it more obvious by asking students to suggest what they could take, or emphasising the first letters of students' names.)

## Numbers

**Numbers quiz**

Here are the answers to some questions. (Write the answers in random order on the board.) Copy them as a list and practise saying them with a partner.

Join another pair and play as a team. I'll ask the questions and the first team to shout out the right answer gets a point.

---

 1 How far is London from Tokyo? (9,562 km)
 2 How far is New York from Buenos Aires? (8,454 km)
 3 What temperate does water boil at? (100°C)
 4 How much of the Earth's surface is covered in water? (almost $^3/_4$)
 5 How many bones are there in the human body? (206)
 6 What is 477 + 345? (822)
 7 What is 1,568 – 744? (824)
 8 How much of the world's electricity is used by America? (33%)
 9 How fast does Concorde fly? (2,333 kph)
10 How fast does a Jumbo jet fly? (963 kph)
11 What is $^1/_3$ as a percentage? (33.3%)
12 How big is the Pacific Ocean? (179,679,000 km$^2$)
13 How high is Mount Kilimanjaro (5,895 m)
14 How high is Mount Cotopaxi (5,896 m)
15 What is the population of the UK? (57,848,000)
16 What is the population of Australia? (19,888,000)

---

**Country statistics**

Work in groups of students from the same country. Agree these statistics for your country. Approximate answers will do.

---

population, population of the capital city, size in km$^2$, highest mountain, longest river, days of sunshine per year, average winter temperature, exchange rate with the US dollar, average monthly salary, income tax rate, cost of a Coca-Cola, cost of a first class stamp

---

(If the class is mixed nationality, reorganise students into mixed nationality groups to compare statistics. If there is a majority from one country, they can double up.)

Tell me how you think your country compares with the UK/USA/Australia. (Ask for comparisons from random students and elicit approximate numbers each time.)

### Arithmetic

How do you say these calculations?

| | | | | |
|---|---|---|---|---|
| $2 + 6 = 8$ | $9 - 4 = 5$ | $3 \times 2 = 6$ | $8 \div 2 = 4$ | $2.5 + 2.5 = 5$ |

We are all going to do a calculation. I'll give you a number to start with. (Choose one less than 10.) Take turns to choose from *plus*, *minus* or *times* and then choose another number less than 10. Don't say the total.

Everybody, write down the calculations and the total after each student's turn. (Continue until everyone has had a turn. With large classes, stop after ten turns and start a new calculation.) Compare your totals. If they are different, who went wrong, and where?

### Number crunching

Give me seven numbers between one and ten. (Write them on the board.) Now say a number between a hundred and five hundred. This is the target number.

In small groups, use the numbers to get as close as possible to the target. You don't have to use all the numbers but you cannot use any number more than once, e.g. 6, 8, 2, 7, 10, 1, 4, target 452. – *Seven times six is forty-two, plus four is forty-six, times ten is four hundred and sixty, minus eight is four hundred and fifty-two.* The group that gets nearest to the target number wins.

### Magic numbers

(Ask the students each to pick a number between 2 and 9 without saying what it is. Then ask them to multiply that number by 9. Next, ask them to add the two digits of the result. Ask them to subtract 5 from this number. Tell them to think of the letter of the alphabet that corresponds to that number: 1 is A, 2 is B, etc. Tell them to think of a country that starts with that letter. Then ask them to pick the next letter of the alphabet, and an animal that starts with that letter. Now tell them you know what they are thinking, and that it is 'Elephants in Denmark'.)

## Parts of the body

### Feet and feats

Listen to these parts of the body and point to them on yourself.

> feet, palm, nails, throat, ears, knuckles, eyes, knees, teeth, tongue, eyelids, lips, fingers, leg, shoulder, thumb

In pairs, suggest a verb for each part of the body and write a sentence, e.g. Feet – *run. They ran onto the platform.*

Swap partners. Take turns to read your sentences and see if your partner can name the part of the body.

### Monsters

In groups, write parts of the body on little pieces of paper. Don't write plurals; if you want two ears, write 'ear' on two pieces of paper. Include a few adjectives on some more pieces of paper, e.g. long, big. (Collect all the pieces of paper, shuffle them and share them out equally between the groups.)

Draw a picture of a monster using all the body parts and adjectives you have received. Add labels to explain mutations, e.g. *One big ear, for listening to the ground.*

Put your pictures up on the wall and have a look at the other groups' pictures.

## Organs

▶ Work in groups and write a list of as many organs as you can think of, e.g. lungs, heart. Pass your list to the next group and add any missing words to the list you receive.

Write a question to elicit each item on the list, e.g. *What do you breathe with?*

▶ How many animal organs have you eaten? What animal did they come from? Make a list of all the animal organs which are edible?

## Body verbs

Work in two groups, A and B. (If the class is large, you can subdivide the groups.) I'll write your group's verbs on the board. For each of your verbs, make a note of which part of the body does it and why people do it. Don't write the verb, e.g. smack – *hand. People sometimes do this to children when they are naughty.*

> Group A: yawn, sneeze, nod, smack, nudge, scratch, sigh, reach, wink, stamp, wave
>
> Group B: pout, kick, shrug, slap, frown, point, hitch-hike, stretch, kneel, weep, rub

Work with a partner from the other group. Read your sentences in random order and see if your partner can guess the verb.

## Body idioms

▶ What does the idiomatic expression *'Get off my back!'* mean?

In groups, tell each other any idioms in your language which use parts of the body. (While they are doing this, write up the word list and the gapfill sentences on the board.)

Fill the gaps with one of these words. Some words can be used more than once. Then discuss what the sentences mean.

> stomach, hair, headless, cheeky, guts, eye, face, hand, legged, eyes, nosy, tooth, elbow
>
> 1 Will you give me a _____ ? I need some help with this door.
> 2 The thieves snatched her bag and _____ it down Oxford Street.
> 3 Let's _____ the facts and be realistic about our options.
> 4 I can't _____ the sight of blood!
> 5 She gave him the _____ because he was making _____ at other girls.
> 6 You _____ little devil! It's rude to talk to adults like that.
> 7 I don't believe in capital punishment: an _____ for an _____ , a _____ for a _____ – it doesn't make sense.
> 8 A – Have you got a boyfriend? B – Don't be so _____ . It's none of your business.
> 9 He's got a lot of _____ taking on the robbers like that. He's very brave.
> 10 It was a _____-raising bus journey along winding mountain roads.
> 11 It was hectic at work. I was running around like a _____ chicken.

Think of a recent time when one of these idioms would have been appropriate for you. Tell the rest of the group.

▶ Draw a person in the middle of a piece of paper. Draw arrows to different parts of the body and for each one write an idiom using that part of the body. (Provide an advanced learner's dictionary for this.) Leave your drawing on the table and look at the other groups' drawings.

## Take after ⚠

In small groups, tell each other who you take after in your family, with reference to your physical characteristics, e.g. *I've got my mother's eyes. I've got big hands like my grandfather.*

**Paths of the heart**

Choose one of these words and look it up in an English-only learner's dictionary: hand, head, foot. Choose some of the words and idioms and arrange them in a network, as in this example for 'heart'.

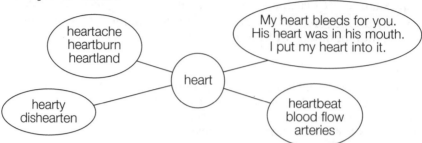

## Phrasal verbs

**Verb chain**

Work in groups of four to six. Take turns to give a phrasal verb, alternately changing the particle and the verb, e.g. A – *Take off.* B – *Take up.* C – *Let up.* D – *Let down.* E – *Put down.* F – *Put on.*

If you can't think of one, you are out of the game. If you doubt another student's phrasal verb, challenge him/her to define it and give an example. If the student can't, he/she is out of the game. (Don't let students write during the activity, but make a note of the most useful phrasal verbs to revise at the end.)

**My mime**

Shout out the phrasal verb I'm miming.

> ask for, get up, come in, look for, take off, fall over, hold on, show off, sit down, fall over, (get) cut off, come back, lean against, cut down, turn round, jump over, throw up, run over, look after, come across, run out of, tell off, look up (a word)

Work in groups and see how many of the phrasal verbs you can remember. Take turns to choose verbs to act out for the rest of the group using mime and words, e.g. come across – *Oh, look! I've found an old coin down the back of this armchair.*

**Turnover**

In groups, write fifteen phrasal verbs on small pieces of paper, with the verb on one piece of paper and the preposition on another. Keep them in two separate piles and swap them with another group. Spread the pieces of paper out on the table and take turns to turn over one preposition and one verb. Score a point if you can use the resulting verb and preposition in a sentence.

(Variation: Students write the verb on one side of the paper and the preposition on the other side. Place the pieces of paper in a pile in the middle of the group, some verb side up and some preposition side up. In their groups, students take turns to guess what is on the other side of each piece of paper. They can not make the same guess as another student. When they have all had a guess, they turn the paper over. Whoever got it correct gets to keep the piece of paper, provided he/she can give a definition of the phrasal verb. If he/she can't, other students can have a go and whoever gets it right, gets to keep the piece of paper. If no one guesses the preposition or verb, it goes to the bottom of the pile. The person at the end with the most pieces of paper is the winner.)

## Literal and non-literal

I U+

(Write these eight pairs of sentences on the board, gapped and the phrasal verbs in random order in a list at the top.) Each pair of sentences uses the same phrasal verb, once literally and once non-literally. In pairs, complete the sentences with the correct form of the phrasal verbs and mark each sentence literal or non-literal.

| | | |
|---|---|---|
| 1 | a) He turned up the heating. | b) He turned up late for the meeting. |
| 2 | a) I looked up the chimney. | b) I looked up his number in the book. |
| 3 | a) Please put out your cigarette. | b) Please put the cat out. |
| 4 | a) I ran into John in the park. | b) I ran into a tree in the park. |
| 5 | a) Hang up your coat and relax. | b) Hang up and try again later. |
| 6 | a) He took off his coat and relaxed. | b) When the plane took off we relaxed. |
| 7 | a) He broke down and cried | b) He broke down the door with a sledgehammer. |
| 8 | a) We got on the first bus that came. | b) We got on well and decided to be friends. |

Discuss the meanings of the non-literal verbs and check your understanding with a dictionary.

Add another five pairs of sentences to your list, one literal and one non-literal. Choose from these verbs and look them up in the dictionary.

get, hold, break, fall, turn, come, go, put, get, let

## Monologues

I U+

▶ Listen to this monologue and write down all the phrasal verbs you hear.

When I *set off* for work this morning my car *broke down*, so I had to take the bus. At the bus stop I *ran into* an old friend called Jason. He'd *come into* some money recently and was *setting up* a business. He offered to *take me on* and I said I'd *think it over*. When I *got into* work the boss, Mrs Pitchfork, *blew up* at me. I was quite *taken aback* by her attitude, but when I *got over* the initial shock I offered to *make up for* being late, saying I would *stay on* after work. Then it *turned out* she was actually angry because a client I had *taken on* had decided to *pull out* of a valuable contract. Mrs Pitchfork said that because the deal had *fallen through* I had *let the whole company down*. She *went on at* me until I finally *ran out of* patience with her. I said I wouldn't *stand for* it any more, and if she wanted to *take out* the company's problems on me she could *lay me off* there and then. I never thought she'd *go through with* it, but she told me to *look for* another job.
I *got on* the phone to Jason and said I wanted to *take him up on* his offer. He told me to *come over* immediately. I met my new colleagues and I think I'll *get on with* them. My line manager *came across* as a great guy and he *took to* me as well. So everything *ended up* OK today. I'm *looking forward* to starting my new job.

Compare your list with a partner to see if he/she got the same number, and the same phrasal verbs. I'll say it again for you to check.

▶ In groups, compose a monologue for one of the following using these phrasal verbs and any others you think fit. Choose one person to do the writing and another to read out your monologue at the end.

A relationship: go out with, fall for, get on (with), fall out (with), make up, chat up, split up, run into, bring up, look after

A telephone conversation: look up, get through to, cut off, put through, go on, run out of, make out, talk about, call back, hang up

A journey: set off, hold up, take off, check in, stop off/over, come back, pick up, get over, hang around, break down, run out of

## Rooms and furniture

### Rooms

► In groups, brainstorm as many rooms as you can in one minute and write them as a list.

Imagine you've just moved from a small flat into a big house. I'm going to read out some pieces of furniture. You only have one of each thing. Decide which is the best room to put them. Write the word next to that room on your list.

> rug, bed, chair, lamp, TV, microwave, hair drier, table, shelf, cupboard, wardrobe, cot, pot plant, curtains, hi-fi, mirror, DVD player, bookshelf, carpet, piano, rubbish bin, filing cabinet, sofa, computer, painting, chest of drawers

Put a tick next to any of the things you've got at your place. Choose your favourite two items and describe them to the group.

► In three groups, brainstorm some things that you might find in these rooms. Group A, the sitting room; Group B, the bedroom; Group C: the kitchen.

Pass your list to the next group and see if you can add anything to the one that is passed to you.

### Realia race

Everybody stand in the middle of the classroom. I'm going to say some adjectives. The first person to call out something in the classroom described by that adjective gets a point. The person with the most points at the end is the winner.

> blue, bright, big, sharp, warm, new, old, square, soft, useful, tiny, yellow, thin, round

### Picture this

Imagine you are sitting in your favourite room at home. Write a very detailed list of everything you can see. Write one of these letters next to each item on your list: F if it is a piece of furniture, A if it is an appliance or fixture or O if it is an ornament.

In pairs, compare your lists. Imagine you are moving into a house together. Agree which items from your lists you would take. Agree on a list of ten items between you.

### Landscape gardens

► Work in small groups and take a large sheet of paper. I am going to describe my garden. Draw the plan. The back of the house is at the top of your page and the end of the garden is at the bottom.

Listen and put things where I tell you. (Draw a large rectangle on the board to represent the shape of the garden. Describe the location of these things.)

> trees, fence, swing, kennel, greenhouse, path, shed, patio, duck pond, flower bed, bird table, gate, hammock

Discuss any changes you would advise me to make. e.g. *You should have the gate nearer the back of the house. You should have another pond near the apple tree.*

► Write a description of your garden or a garden you know. Describe it in as much detail as you can, including information about the plants, furniture, water features, etc. Read your description to another student.

## Compound nouns

Work in two teams to play noughts and crosses. Take turns to choose a square. To win it you have to make a compound noun with the word in the square, e.g. ash – *tray.*

| | | |
|---|---|---|
| bed | key | table |
| dish | house | door |
| bath | window | book |

doorway – He stood in the doorway and ...
doorman – I asked the doorman at the ...
outdoors/indoors
He was at death's door, starving and ...

Look up the words in the noughts and crosses grid in a learners' dictionary. Make a note of any useful expressions, and write examples.

## Shops

### Commodities

I'm going to read out a list of everyday items. Work in pairs and make a note of where you can buy them, e.g. Pencil – *a stationers.*

some slippers, some roses, a phone card, a packet of cigarettes, a packet of crisps, a magazine, a jacket, a CD, some aspirin, some rope, a dining table, a bottle of wine, a light bulb, an apple, a bag of charcoal, a plain croissant, a ham and cheese croissant, a leg of lamb, a dictionary, a tin of paint, a notepad, a blanket, some ice, a rabbit

### Department stores

In groups, you have two minutes to brainstorm a list of departments in a department store and two things that can be bought in each department.

Decide which floor your departments are on. Then pair up with a student from another group.

Student A, imagine you are in a department store trying to find some of the things on your list. Ask student B where to go.

Student B, tell student A where to go, including directions via the lift/escalator.

Then swap roles.

### Shopping spree

► Tell a partner about the last time you went to these places. Where was it? What did you buy or do?

street market, supermarket, flea market, boutique

► Imagine you have €100 to spend on shopping, and just fifteen minutes to spend it. You must spend all of it. Where are you going to go around here to spend it, and what are you going to buy?

**Amenities**

► In small groups, brainstorm some places where you can do these things.

> listen to music, watch sport, find out about history, take your granny,
> look at art, keep fit, do evening classes, take a child, read a book

Tell each other about the last time you did each thing, e.g. where you went, who you were with, etc.

► In small groups, agree on a list of the ten most important amenities for making a town an enjoyable place to live.

**City streets**

I've got a list of twenty-one things you can see on a city street, apart from shops and other buildings. In two teams, take turns to guess the things on my list and score a point every time you get one correct.

> beggar, bicycle, bus stop, busker, car, dog, drain, graffiti, lamppost, litter, lorry, motorbike,
> pedestrian, phone box, pigeon, postbox, rubbish bin, signpost, traffic lights, tree, taxi

## Spelling

**Missing vowels**

The vowels are missing from this sentence. What does it say? (The next train at platform seven is the six fifteen to Oxford.)

> Th nxt trn t pltfrm svn s th sx fftn t xfrd

In pairs, write another sentence without vowels for another pair to write out in full.

Look back through the vocabulary notes that you have made in recent lessons and choose ten words. Write them without vowels and test your partner.

**Add a letter**

Work in groups of four or five. Take turns to add a letter to a word to make another word. The first letter depends on the number that you throw with a die: 1 = a; 2 = e; 3 = i; 4 = o; 5 = u; 6 = choose a consonant

Score as many points as there are in the word you make. When no one can make the word any longer, start again, e.g.

A throws 4 (o) and adds *n* to make *on* (2 points)
B – adds *o* to make *one* (3 points)
C – adds *l* to make *lone* (4 points)
D – adds *a* to make *alone* (5 points)
E – Can't go so throws again.

Write down the longest three words you make and pass them to the next group. Take turns to shrink the words that are passed to you, subtracting one letter at a time.

**Air words**

Write a list of some recently learnt vocabulary. Working in pairs, sit opposite each other and spell out your words in the air with your finger. Say the words your partner spells.

## Spelling auction

Work in teams. You have €500 to spend on the vocabulary in this list. I'll auction each word. Bid against the other teams. Unfortunately, some of the words are badly spelt and are in fact worth nothing. At the end, the team with the highest number of correctly spelt words is the winner. In the event of a draw, the team with the most money left wins.

(Here is a selection of words. The correct spellings are given in brackets.)

> accross (across), necessary, bicause (because), foreign, iether (either), forty, buisness (business), receipt, government, Wendesday (Wednesday), people, adress (address), tommorow (tomorrow), biscuit, begining (beginning), yesterday, beautifull (beautiful), neighbour, restorant (restaurant), cigarrette (cigarette), sentence

## Grid wars

(Select 25 recently learnt vocabulary items and write the initial letters of each word in the grid.) Work in two teams. Team A has to win a line of letters from top to bottom. Team B has to win a line of letters from left to right. The line can go in any direction, but not diagonally. The teams take turns to choose a letter. I'll give you a definition of a word that begins with that letter. If you guess the word, you win that square. If you get it wrong, the other team gets a go. If they get it right, they win it. If not, the letter is out of bounds. Once a square has been won or gone out of bounds, no team can choose it.

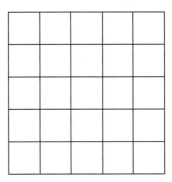

## Word track

Play in groups of three. Copy this grid and write a five-letter word in the middle. Take turns to add a letter, making new words. Score one point for each letter in the new words you make. Look at this example. The starting word is *TABLE*.

Player 1 adds C and gets *cable* and *cat* – eight points. He/She doesn't get any points for *able, at* or *tab* because they don't include the C. Player 2 adds K and gets *back* and *tack* – eight points.

If you spot a word a player has missed, you get the points for that word. Player 2 notices *cab* – three extra points.

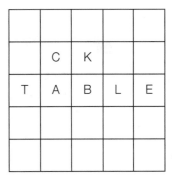

## Wordsearch

Work in pairs and see how many words you can make from the letters in *Wordsearch*.

> ace, ache, acre, adore, arch, archer, are, arrow, awe, car, card, care, case, cash, chase, chew, chord, chore, chose, coarse, cod, code, cord, core, cow, coward, crash, crew, crow, crowd, dare, dash, dear, décor, dew, does, dose, draw, drawer, drew, each, ear, era, had, hard, hare, has, head, hear, heard, her, herd, hero, hoard, horse, hose, how, oar, order, ore, owe, race, rare, rash, raw, reach, read, rear, record, red, reward, road, roar, rode, roe, rose, row, sad, scar, scare, score, screw, sea, search, sew, shade, share, shed, shoe, shore, show, shower, shred, shrew, shrewd, soar, soda, sore, sow, swear, sword, swore, wade, war, ward, ware, was, wash, washer, wear, wed, who, whose, word, wore, worse

(For higher level classes.) Join another pair. Use your words in a short story.

**Code words**

In groups, look back through your notes and select twenty words that you have learnt. Write them as a list, but jumble the letters up so that each word is an anagram, e.g. message – *esgames*. Write a clue for each word, e.g. *The first letter is 'm'; it's a noun.*

Pass your list to another group. Can you unjumble the words that are passed to your group?

**Spellbound**

Take turns to say a word. The only rules are: 1) Your word must include the letter C. 2) You may not say the same word that another student has already said. (Any student who can't give a word is out of the game, and the winner is the last student left.)

(When most of the students have had a go, change the first rule and then change it regularly. Here are some rules. If the class find this too easy, you could give them several rules at the same time.)

---

1   a word including the letter C
2   a word including two vowels
3   a word including the letter S
4   a word with two consonants together
5   a word with a double letter
6   a word with two or more syllables
7   a word including the letter H
8   a word ending with the letter D
9   a word containing at least three different vowels
10  a word with a silent letter

---

(Variation: Stipulate a part of speech, e.g. An adjective including the letter C.)

## Sports

**Favourite sports**

Look at this diagram. What's the sport and what categories do the circles represent? (Answer: cricket. Equipment, places, events, outstanding competitors and rules.)

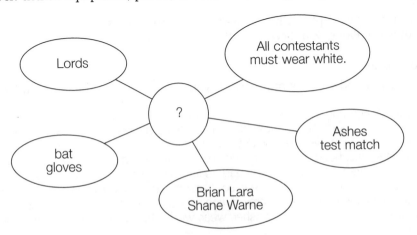

Work in groups of students who have the same favourite sport and make a similar diagram for your sport. Don't write the category names. Swap diagrams with another group to guess the categories.

## Serve and volley

Work in groups of three. Choose a sport and take turns to give a related word, e.g. tennis –
*serve, court, love.* The last person to think of a word gets a point and chooses the next sport.
Proper nouns are not allowed.

> football, squash, boxing, skiing, baseball, hockey,
> formula 1, basketball, athletics, cycling, golf, cricket

## Categories

Choose one of these headings and write a list of different sports. Write a few notes
describing any experience you have had of playing or watching them, e.g. football –
*last Saturday in the park.*

> winter sports, decathlon, water sports, animal sports, table sports,
> motor sports, ball sports, fighting sports, extreme sports

In pairs, compare your lists, and tell each other about your experiences.

# Time

## Dates

► In pairs, listen to these questions and write the dates down in words, e.g. *the twenty-fifth
of December.*

> 1  What's the date today?
> 2  What was the date yesterday?
> 3  What date was it last Tuesday?
> 4  What's the date on Thursday?
> 5  What date was it last Thursday?
>
> 6  What was the date three weeks ago today?
> 7  What are the dates of this course/term?
> 8  What's the date the day after tomorrow?
> 9  What date is the next exam?
> 10 What date will it be a week on Saturday?

Compare your answers with another pair.

► I'm going to dictate the dates of the astrological signs. Make a note of the signs and
the dates, in numbers, e.g. *Aries: 21/3 – 20/4.*

> Aries: 21 Mar – 20 Apr      Taurus: 21 Apr – 21 May      Gemini: 22 May – 22 Jun
> Cancer: 23 Jun – 23 Jul     Leo: 24 Jul – 23 Aug         Virgo: 24 Aug – 23 Sep
> Libra: 24 Sep – 23 Oct      Scorpio: 24 Oct – 22 Nov     Sagittarius: 23 Nov – 21 Dec
> Capricorn: 22 Dec – 20 Jan  Aquarius: 21 Jan – 19 Feb    Pisces: 20 Feb – 20 Mar

Take turns to tell me your sign and when the sign is, e.g. *My sign is Aries. That's from the
twenty-first of March to the twentieth of April.*

## Clocks

(Draw three clock faces on the board, each showing a different time. Ask different students
at random to say the times. Then tell them that the clocks are fast by twenty minutes.
Elicit the new times. Change the times again and continue until everyone has had a few
goes. If the class is mixed nationality, ask them what the time is in their home towns.)

## Important dates

▶ Work in small groups. Tell each other about some important dates in your country's history.

When are these celebrations?

| | |
|---|---|
| Christmas Day (25th December) | Guy Fawkes Night (5th November) |
| April Fool's Day (1st April) | St Valentine's Day (14th February) |
| Independence Day in the USA (4th July) | New Year's Eve (31st December) |
| Midsummer's Day (21st June) | Halloween (31st October) |

Compare your answers with another group.

▶ Work in small groups. Write down these dates as a list on the left of your paper. (Dictate the dates in brackets below.).

Listen to these historic events, and write them next to the correct dates. (Read them out in random order.)

The D-Day landings happened in Normandy. (6th June 1944)
Neil Armstrong was the first man to walk on the Moon. (20th July 1969)
Christopher Columbus reached the West Indies. (12th October 1492)
John F Kennedy was assassinated. (22nd November 1963)
The first telephone call was made. (6th March 1876) .
There was a terrorist attack on the Twin Towers, New York. (11th September 2001)
The Wright brothers made the first powered flight. (17th December 1903)
Yuri Gegarin was the first man in space. (12th April 1961)
William the Conqueror invaded England. (14th October 1066)
The Soviet Union officially ended. (25th December 1991)

Compare your answers with another group.

## Personal time

▶ In pairs, ask and answer questions about these things. (If students have got children, they can talk about them instead.)

the day you were born, the time of day you were born, the month you were born, the season you were born, the year you were born, the decade you were born

▶ In pairs, ask and answer questions using this table.

| What do you do | in the morning in the afternoon at night | on | Sundays? Wednesdays? Saturdays? Christmas day? |
|---|---|---|---|
| | | | |

▶ Carry out a survey of the rest of the class. Choose one of these subjects and find out how long each student spends doing it each day. Make a list, with those who spend the most time at the top and those who spend the least at the bottom.

watching TV, sleeping, eating, sitting on public transport, exercising, speaking on the phone, cooking, walking, relaxing, reading, drinking tea or coffee, studying, using a computer

Report some of your results to the class. (Elicit the extremes.)

## What time do you …?

When you hear these words, quickly make a question about what time I do the thing, e.g. train – *What time do you catch the train to work?* Make a note of my answers. (Answer two questions with lies and the rest truthfully.)

> work/lesson, get up, lunch break, home, bed, breakfast, bus/train

Two of my answers were lies. In pairs, decide which ones.

In pairs, ask each other questions in the same way, e.g. A – *What time do you get up?* B – *I get up at eleven.*

## Duration

Put these time periods in order, from the shortest to the longest.

> an hour, a century, a decade, a week, a year, a month, a second, a minute, a day, a season, a millennium

Write a *How long …?* question for five of them and take turns to ask your partner, e.g. A – *How long is one year?* B – *A year is 365 days.*

In pairs, write some more questions with *How long does it take (you) to … ?* Make sure you both have a copy of the questions, then swap partners and ask your new partner your questions, e.g. A – *How long does it take to boil an egg?* B – *It takes four minutes.*

## Time-saving devices

In small groups, brainstorm ten time-saving devices we use for doing ordinary jobs. Put them in order from the most to the least useful. Compare lists with another group.

## Weather

## Seasons

▶ (Divide the class into groups of four and allocate one season to each group.) In your groups, brainstorm sentences to describe the seasons in the UK, e.g. *In spring the birds start to sing. The flowers come out.*

Group A, write about the spring. Group B, write about the summer. Group C, write about the autumn. Group D, write about the winter.

Pass your description to the next group and see if you can add to the one that is passed to your group.

Tell your group something you like and something you dislike about each season, e.g. *I like the way the days get longer in spring.*

Compare the seasons in your country with those in the UK/USA/Australia. (If it's a mixed nationality class, ask them to find comparisons between their countries, e.g. *In my country, it's much colder in the winter. There are more mosquitoes in the summer.*)

▶ Work in two teams. Listen to this list of words. For each one, shout out which season in the UK it belongs to. The first team to answer correctly wins a point.

> snow, sunbathing, planting flowers, icicles, ice-cream, hot, cool, cuckoo, darkness, birds, rain, migration, thunder, April showers, red leaves, football, camping, harvest, cricket, lambs, skiing, mushrooms, central heating, fog, barbecues, daffodils, long nights

**Weather words**

On your own, write some words that you associate with the sun, rain and snow, e.g. *sun – beach, volleyball, holiday, Greece*. Compare your lists with a partner, explaining why you chose your words and places.

**Weather forecast**

► (Draw pictures on the board to elicit *rain, sun, wind, cloud, snow* and *fog*.)

In pairs, copy this table and add as many expressions as you can.

| Noun | Adjective | Verb |
|------|-----------|------|
| rain | *It's rainy.* <br> *It's a rainy country.* | *It's raining.* <br> *It rains a lot here.* |
| sun <br> wind <br> cloud <br> snow <br> fog | | |

► In pairs, discuss these questions.

> What is the weather forecast for the next couple of days?
> What kinds of weather are typical at different times of the year?
> What are the points of the compass and the points in between?

Work in five groups and write a weather forecast for these parts of the UK. Decide what kind of weather you want first. (Make sure that a wide variety is included between the five groups, e.g. snow in the Highlands of Scotland and warm sunshine in the south.)

Group A – East Anglia and the south-east
Group B – The south and south-west
Group C – Wales and Northern Ireland
Group D – The Midlands and the north-east
Group E – Scotland and the north of England

(Draw a map of the UK on the board. Ask one student to come to the board. The five groups take turns to give their forecasts and the student at the board draws weather icons accordingly.)

(Variation: Change the location to the country the class are studying in.)

**Natural disasters**

Tell me some different kinds of natural disaster, and a recent example of one that has happened in the world.

> flood, drought, forest fire, tidal wave, hurricane, avalanche, earthquake, volcanic eruption

In small groups, discuss these questions.

> What happens when each of these natural disasters occurs?
> Are any of them a result of human activity?
> How is the global climate changing?

Tell each other about the most severe weather or natural event you have experienced.

## Storyboard

I'm going to tell you a story, but without speaking. I'll draw on the board and mime. You tell me each line of the story. If it's correct, I'll nod and you can write it down.

> It was a beautiful morning. The sun was shining and the birds were singing. I got up early, had breakfast and took the dog for a walk along the beach. After an hour or so it got cloudy and the wind started blowing. I turned for home but got caught in a heavy downpour. Then the thunder and lighting started. The waves on the sea got higher and higher.

In small groups, continue the story, e.g. *The storm got a lot worse.*

Tell the rest of your group about a time you got caught in bad weather.

## Word association

## Adjectives

Stand in a circle. Take turns to throw a ball to each other and follow this sequence: 1) say an adjective; 2) say an associated noun; 3) make a sentence with the adjective and noun, and so on, e.g.

A (throwing) – *Green.*
B (catching) – *Tree.*
C (catching) – *The trees are very green in the summer.*
D (catching) – *Hot …*

(Variation: Students only have to say adjectives, but they must begin with the last letter of the previous adjective, e.g. *green, **new**, wonderful, **lovely** …*)

## Collocations

In pairs, think of an appropriate adjective to follow these adverbs, e.g. devilishly – *hot*. (Suggested answers are shown in brackets. Don't give them out at this stage.)

> smartly (dressed); dearly (loved); securely (fastened, tied), widely (known,scattered, accepted); heavily (built, guarded, defeated, pregnant); seriously (injured, ill, concerned); brightly (lit, coloured); randomly (selected) wildly (exited, exaggerated); stunningly (beautiful)

Compare your ideas with another pair.

I'm going to read out the adjectives on my list. Decide which adverbs they go with. (Read them out in a different order.)

Write a short story using at least five of the adverb/adjective combinations.

## Pairs

(Do this as an open class activity.) I will say a word. Shout out the word that goes with it, e.g. T – *bread and …* S – *butter!*

> socks, knives, sweet, cats, bacon, war, salt, left, high, son, pen, right, fish, sun, black, hands, gin, here, bread, over, thunder, husband, heaven, rock

Work in three teams. Write as many of the pairs as you can from memory. The team that remembers the most is the winner.

**Links**

Look at this word association chain.

> book – write – pen – ink – octopus – legs – run – bus –
> ticket – cinema – Hollywood – actor – play – game …

Suggest some connections between the words, e.g. *Ink is the stuff you put in a pen.*

In groups, continue the chain. You can say anything but you have to explain the connection if someone queries it.

**Think of a use**

Work in pairs. Make connections by saying what the things in the first column can do with the things in the second, e.g. *A mouse can use a brick to hide behind.*

> mouse, waiter, baby, doctor, teacher, monkey, wife, farmer, you, prisoner

> apple, brick, cup, egg, piece of string, fork, skis, dog, bottle, bar of soap

When you have finished, swap partners with another pair and compare the way you connected things.

**Throw it out**

Work in groups of four. Choose a letter each: A, B, C and D. I'm going to read out some sets of four words. A takes the first, B the second, etc. Discuss who does not belong in the group each time. Try to persuade your group that you should stay in. You have a minute before I read the next set of words, e.g. tomato, orange, potato, onion. S – *We decided to throw out the potato because it's the most boring.*

> 1  garden, flower, grass, tree
> 2  book, page, line, word
> 3  hat, scarf, shirt, gloves
> 4  piano, guitar, cello, trumpet
> 5  I, we, him, they
> 6  blue, green, red, yellow
> 7  iron, copper, brass, gold
> 8  iron, mop, hoover, broom
> 9  skinny, slender, lithe, thin
> 10  wire, where, wear, ware
> 11  in, on, up, opposite
> 12  table, chair, cooker, sofa

**Opposites**

I am going to read out some words. Shout out the opposites. You may have to explain why you think they are opposites. When you have had a go, keep quiet until everyone else has had one.

> admit, awake, beautiful, big, black, cheer, dawn, dirty, dry, empty, fast, few, float, here, high, hot, huge, melt, near, never, nice, old, plural, smooth, some, still, sunny, sweet, tall, tame, tender, up, warm, will, win

**Parts**

Work in pairs. Agree what these things are part of, e.g. page – *book*.

> leg, uncle, house, day, verb, star, wheel, MP, fork, modem, bone, word, soldier, student, wave, minute, bird, tree, brick

Choose a few of the words and see how many more words you can add to them, e.g. page – *book – collection – library – university.*

# Index